AMAZING ADVENTURES CREATIVE CONNECTIONS AND DARING DEEDS

AMAZING ADVENTURES CREATIVE CONNECTIONS AND DARING DEEDS

40 IDEAS THAT PUT FEET TO YOUR FAMILY'S FAITH

TIM AND ALISON SIMPSON

NAVPRESS

Discipleship Inside Out™

NavPress is the publishing ministry of The Navigators, an international Christian organization and leader in personal spiritual development. NavPress is committed to helping people grow spiritually and enjoy lives of meaning and hope through personal and group resources that are biblically rooted, culturally relevant, and highly practical.

For a free catalog go to www.NavPress.com
or call 1.800.366.7788 in the United States or 1.800.839.4769 in Canada.

© 2010 by Tim and Alison Simpson

ISBN-13: 978-1-60006-624-5

Cover design by Arvid Wallen

Some of the anecdotal illustrations in this book are true to life and are included with the permission of the persons involved. All other illustrations are composites of real situations, and any resemblance to people living or dead is coincidental.

Unless otherwise identified, all Scripture quotations in this publication are taken from the *Holy Bible, New International Version* (NIV). Copyright © 1973, 1978, 1984 by International Bible Society. Used by permission of Zondervan. All rights reserved. Other versions used include: the *Contemporary English Version* (CEV) copyright © 1995 by American Bible Society. Used by permission; and *THE MESSAGE* (MSG). Copyright © 1993, 1994, 1995, 1996, 2000, 2001, 2002. Used by permission of NavPress Publishing Group.

Library of Congress Cataloging-in-Publication Data

Simpson, Tim.
  Amazing adventures, creative connections, and daring deeds : 40 ideas that put feet to your family's faith / Tim and Alison Simpson.
    p. cm.
  ISBN 978-1-60006-624-5
  1. Families--Religious life. 2. Christian life--Biblical teaching. 3. Christian education--Home training. I. Simpson, Alison, 1966- II. Title.
  BV4526.3.S513 2010
  248.8'45--dc22
                              2009052646

Printed in the United States of America

1 2 3 4 5 6 7 8 / 14 13 12 11 10

For Sam and Anna

CONTENTS

INTRODUCTION:
A PLACE TO
EXPERIENCE JESUS

What if your family became a place where you could experience Jesus?

We wrote this book to help your family do just that. While churches can be terrific places to find community and support, the way we live out our faith comes mostly from within our homes. What we learn at church pales in comparison to what we learn at home through what family members say and how they behave.

The concept of this book sprung from an "accident." One year we learned that a friend of ours was going to spend Christmas alone, and we just couldn't let that happen. We invited our friend over and bought presents and filled a stocking for our special guest. We learned what a gift it was for us to celebrate our Savior's birth with someone who would not have done so otherwise. Our family wasn't intentional when we reached out to our friend, but because of that, we began to explore other ways we could intentionally grow in our faith and reach beyond ourselves . . . to "put feet to our faith."

Whether your family is just beginning your journey of following Jesus or is further along that road, whether it has two parents or one, is comprised of grandparents taking care of grandchildren, or is a group of singles who are your family of friends, the family is your number one teacher. The discussions and adventures in this book provide the opportunity to live out Jesus' teachings and to experience loving, caring, and giving together in family life. All of the activities can be adapted to fit your needs. Feel free to be creative and adjust them to something that will work better for your situation.

Each chapter has a "Reaching In" activity that draws you into the subject. These are designed to be active and creative, so go all out! Next, the "Reaching Into the Word" section explores what the Bible has to say about the topic and how your family can apply it to life. This section also has age-appropriate questions; however, the age specified is only a guideline. Feel free to use different questions depending on your children's development. The final section, "Reaching Into the World," takes what you've just learned and moves your family out into your community at large, where you'll reach out to others in innovative and meaningful ways.

Don't be surprised if over time, as you serve, give, and love together, you begin to see those Christlike qualities spill over into your family's everyday routine. You may also find that doing life together through these amazing adventures dramatically brings your family closer together—the way Jesus meant for your family to be.

1

THE BIG GIVE

And he said, "I tell you that this poor woman has put in more than all the others."

— LUKE 21:3 (CEV)

With mortgages to pay, high energy costs, taxes, and countless other financial obligations, families can find it difficult to give generously. Regardless of these pressures, a family that sacrifices and gives generously will reap dividends far beyond whatever monetary loss it experiences. When children see their parents selflessly giving of their money, time, and resources, they learn to orient their own lives the same way. Parents will experience the joy that giving can bring to their own individual souls, and to the collective spirit of the family. When a family learns to put others first and to give, it beautifully transforms the culture of the household.

REACHING IN

Gather your family and ask everyone to find their most prized possession and bring it back for "show and tell." If it's impractical to bring the item to the meeting place (such as a car or backyard pool), have the family member bring something to represent it, such as car keys or a swimsuit. Then have everyone show their prized possession and answer the following questions:

- Why did you choose this as your most prized possession?
- How difficult would it be to give it away to help someone in need?

We don't like to think about giving up the things we love most because it often feels as if we're giving up security, status, and comfort. Ironically, doing so can move us toward a greater reliance on Christ, who gives us true and ultimate security, status, and comfort.

REACHING INTO THE WORD — LUKE 21:1-4

Look up Luke 21:1-4 and read the story. Then answer the following questions:

For ages 4–7
- What did the widow do that impressed Jesus so much?
- What are some ways you can give?

For ages 8–10
- Why did Jesus think the widow had given more than the others?
- How can you give like the widow?

For ages 11–13
- What point did Jesus make about giving?
- Why is it sometimes hard for people to give like the widow?

For ages 14 and up
- What does this story teach us about the difference between sacrificial giving and other kinds of giving?
- How does sacrificial giving change us?

Look again at the prized possessions you gathered earlier. Imagine what it would be like to sacrifice those things if you believed Jesus was asking you to do so. How would it feel to lose them? What would it feel like to keep them in spite of Christ's call to sacrifice them? Do you think that as a family you are open to letting go of anything Jesus asks you to? Explain your answer.

REACHING INTO THE WORLD

Most towns have a place to donate food for redistribution to the poor and hungry. You'll often find different businesses or organizations setting up food drives and asking people to bring in cans of food or some other nonperishable items. Your family's mission is to pack up and give away every bit of nonperishable food in your house. That's right, *all of it.* Pack up all of your canned goods and unopened boxes of food and take them as a family to your local church or another organization that runs a food distribution center.

After the delivery, ask God to use the food given to further His kingdom. Ask Him to continually teach your family to be sacrificial givers and to give you the faith to do so when this stretches your finances.

Sacrificial giving can bring your family closer together and teach you to be selfless with each other and the world, which is what the Christ-centered life is all about.

2.

BFF (BEST FRIENDS FOREVER)

A friend loves at all times,
and a brother is born for adversity.

— PROVERBS 17:17

In the movie *Cast Away*, Tom Hanks' character, Chuck Noland, is stranded on a deserted island after a terrible plane crash. In his desperation for companionship, Chuck creates a friend out of a volleyball, which he names "Wilson." Chuck paints a face on the ball, gives it hair, and carries it everywhere. He constantly discusses options and decisions with the ball. It's the only way he can cope with his loneliness.

While we might chuckle at the idea of relating to a ball as if it were our friend, this movie illustrates a universal truth: People need people. Everyone needs friends. They make us laugh, and they help us through challenges. They cry with us when we're sad, and they listen to us when we need to talk. They support us and work together with us, and as a result, we are stronger. When we have friends, it makes the bad times a little easier and the great times even better.

REACHING IN

Send your family members on a quest through your house to gather pictures of friends. Bring them to your kitchen table, living room, or wherever you have the space for this activity. Spread out all your pictures and take a minute to look at them. Share with each other any memories the pictures might remind you of. Talk about what makes those people special to you.

Next, answer these questions:

For ages 4–7
- Who is your best friend?
- How do best friends treat each other?

For ages 8–10
- How do you make friends?
- How do you keep a friendship strong?

For ages 11–13
- How do you know when someone is a real friend?
- How have you been a real friend?

For ages 14 and up
- What are the qualities of a good friendship?
- Why is it sometimes difficult to be a good friend?

Pair up with another member of your family and act out something (like you might while playing Charades) that shows one quality of a good friend. See if the others can guess what you're acting out. Do as many as you have time for.

REACHING INTO THE WORD — PROVERBS 17:17

The book of Proverbs is a collection of ancient Hebrew sayings thought to be wise words to live by. It's filled with advice for both young and old, rich and poor, powerful and helpless. It also has something to say about friendship and families.

Take a look at this paraphrase of Proverbs 17:17 from *The Message*: "Friends love through all kinds of weather, and families stick together in all kinds of trouble."

Everyone — big and small, young and old — needs friendship. However, this verse isn't just talking about "fair-weather friends"; it's talking about the people who help you through hard times and challenges. That's the kind of friend we all need.

Put the pictures of your friends on your refrigerator. As you do, say a one-sentence prayer for each person. Leave up the photos as a reminder to always be a Proverbs 17:17 friend and to pray for your friends on a regular basis.

REACHING INTO THE WORLD

Plan a BFF party that honors all of your friends for their support and love. Serve great food, plan fun games, and display pictures of times you've shared with them. Put together gift bags for everyone and include a personal note, thanking each person for specific ways he or she has meant so much to your family.

3

THE GIFT OF DIRECTION

Show me your paths and teach me to follow.
— PSALM 25:4 (CEV)

Whether you are doing something as simple as driving your car or as life-altering as making a career change, knowing what direction to go takes a real load off the brain. On the flip side, not knowing which way to go, or being lost, can bring on stress, confusion, anxiety, fear, and panic.

God created us to follow Christ's direction. When we go against the way He designed, we can experience, in the most profound way, all those terrible emotions that go along with being lost. We've all been there from time to time. We've all tried to find our own way and have ignored God's direction for us.

Many of us have been blessed by a friend, a mentor, or even a stranger helping us get back on the right path of trusting Jesus and following His lead. As a family, you can do the same for someone else.

REACHING IN

Find a road map of your town, state, or country. Sit down as a family and find a place you enjoy going or would like to go. Use a highlighter to mark the best route for getting there. Discuss the following questions:

- What would it be like to find a place you've never been without a map?
- How does God act as a map for us as a family?

REACHING INTO THE WORD — PSALM 25:1-10

Those who don't walk with Christ are "lost" in life because they are without His direction. To better understand what this is like, have everyone find a pillowcase or some other cloth to use for a blindfold. Take turns blindfolding each other and then trying to walk around your home with no help. Then take turns again, this time with someone guiding you. When you are finished, read Psalm 25:1-10 and answer the following questions:

For ages 4–7
- How does it feel when someone guides us?
- How does it feel when God guides us?

For ages 8–10
- How does it feel to be guided instead of trying to do something alone?
- What are some ways we can trust God and let Him guide us?

For ages 11–14
- Why do people sometimes refuse the guidance of others?
- Why do people sometimes refuse to trust God to guide them?

For ages 14 and up
- When have you stumbled without guidance and wished someone had reached out to help you?
- In the Scripture passage, the psalmist asked God for guidance. Why is it sometimes hard for you to do that?

Feeling lost and alone is a horrible feeling. We panic, make poor choices, and grasp desperately for anything that looks safe, even when it's not. This isn't just true for individuals, but also for families. Seeking guidance from Jesus won't automatically give you a clear picture of what to do, but He will take care of you and keep you on the right track. Pray for God to guide your family and for you to have the faith to rely on Him.

REACHING INTO THE WORLD

More than any other age group, teenagers typically are seen as the ones most in need of guidance. Yet, often they are also the most difficult group to convince that they need guidance. What can your family do to help the teens whom you know?

Think of a teen in your church or community who might be in need of some guidance or a family to connect with. Go shopping for a gift for him or her, such as a Christian CD. Then invite that teen out for dinner or to your house for a home-cooked meal. Spend the evening playing games and visiting, and present the gift to the teen. End the evening by praying together with the teen, thanking God for him or her and for the fun time you had together, and asking for direction in the teen's life.

4

LOVE COMES DOWN

*Think how much the Father loves us. He loves us so much
that he lets us be called his children.*

— I JOHN 3:1 (CEV)

Without food, we'd die of starvation. Without water, we'd die of
dehydration. Without shelter, we'd die of exposure. And without
love, we'd die emotionally from the trauma of life. The lack of love
in people's lives is the cause of so many tragedies. The prostitute
who never experienced the loving arms of caring people sells herself
in a sad and desperate attempt to find the love her soul craves. The
Wall Street executive hoards more and more money, trying to fill up
an empty life with what only love can truly satisfy.

Ideally, your family overflows with love. Families who love each
other let all of the members be themselves, and they expect family
members to conduct themselves in a caring way toward everyone.
In Christian families the love of Jesus radiates out to others, both
in and beyond the family.

REACHING IN

Gather for a brief scavenger hunt. Ask each person to find two items from around the house. One should represent love within your family. The other should represent God's love for your family. Once everyone has come back together, ask each person to show his or her items and explain why he or she chose them. Discuss the following questions:

- Why is it so important as a family to love each other and God?
- How can we as a family do better at this over the next few days?

REACHING INTO THE WORD — 1 JOHN 3:1

So many people come from broken or dysfunctional homes. But regardless of what we may wish our nuclear families could have done differently, 1 John 3:1 gives us a beautiful visual of a loving family with God as the father. It can bring great comfort to know that we are part of His family, where loving each other is key.

Take a look at 1 John 3:1 and then answer the following questions:

For ages 4–7
- How does it feel to be part of God's family?
- Show with your arms just how much God loves you.

For ages 8–10
- What does being part of God's family mean to you?
- How does God's love for you help you throughout the day?

For ages 11–13
- Is being part of God's family a comfort to you or something else? Why?
- Is it sometimes hard to believe that God really loves you? Why?

For ages 14 and up
- How does being part of God's family change the way you approach life?
- How can God's love heal the hurts that life sometimes brings us?

Members of a family are to love each other and to understand that they are part of the larger family of God. His love can overflow out of our hearts and be felt by everyone that comes in contact with us.

REACHING INTO THE WORLD

Love is foundational to healthy living. God designed us to love God and to love our family. In this activity, we encourage you to take the love you have for each other and shower it on someone in need. Showing another person what love looks like is the most Christlike thing we can do.

Think of a family that is new to your church. Put together a welcome package for them that includes coupons, food, a church directory (or telephone book if they're new to town), handmade gifts from your kids, and anything else you can think of that would be helpful and encouraging. Write a note saying how glad you are that they are a part of your church family. Arrange a time to deliver your package and introduce your family to theirs.

THE LOOK OF LOVE

When I was hungry, you gave me something to eat, and
when I was thirsty, you gave me something to drink.
When I was a stranger, you welcomed me.

— MATTHEW 25:35 (CEV)

You can tell a great teacher by how his or her students put into practice what they learned. Great teachers are behind many successful people.

Jesus taught us how to love, and it's our role to put into practice what He taught us. He demonstrated to us what perfect love looks like by coming to earth and showing us how to love. In an ultimate act of love, He died on the cross to save us from our lack of love. He taught us that we should show through our actions what love looks like.

If you have ever been a part of meeting basic human needs for another person, then you know how meeting that need can show love — and that doing so often changes you as well. Because this requires looking inward as well as looking outward to the needs of others, families that love others begin to act differently, see the world differently, and love on a deeper level than was possible before.

REACHING IN

Find a sugar-cookie recipe, a heart-shaped cookie cutter, cookie ingredients, and cookie-decorating supplies (icing, sprinkles, and so on). Meet your family in the kitchen for a fun time of making cookies. Then, while the cookies bake, discuss the following questions:

- When have you seen love on display recently?
- When have you recently shown what love looks like?
- How can we use these cookies to show others what love looks like?

After the cookies finish baking, decorate them with love as your theme.

REACHING INTO THE WORD — MATTHEW 25:35-40

Matthew 25:35-40 is famous for being one of the most pointed and challenging of Jesus' teachings. In it He implored us to practice showering the world with His love, just as He taught us. He insisted that we be an extension of His love to those around us.

Read the passage and choose one of the following activities appropriate to your children's ages.

For families with children 9 and under

Parents (and children 10 and older) will act out being hungry, then thirsty, then alone or like a stranger, then naked (but not actually naked, just acting how it would feel to be naked!), then sick, and then in jail. Have children under 10 years old figure out how to help in each situation. Then discuss the following questions:

- What was it like to help someone in need?
- How did the kind actions show what love looks like?

Close in prayer, asking God to help your family show the world what love looks like through your actions.

For families with children 10 and up

As a family, search the Internet for ways that Christians have helped those who are hungry, thirsty, alone, in need of clothing, sick, and in jail. Then discuss the following questions:

- How did these Christians help those in need beyond just feeding them, clothing them, and so on?
- What are some ways your family can show what love looks like by helping people who are hungry, thirsty, alone, in need of clothes, sick, or in jail?

Close by asking God to help your family show the world what love looks like through your actions.

REACHING INTO THE WORLD

Now it's time for your family to show what love looks like. Take the sugar cookies you baked, box them up, and deliver them to someone who is lonely or in need. Visit with that person for a while and let God's love flow through you.

After you're done with your adventure, pray for the person you visited and ask God to keep giving you opportunities to show the world what love looks like.

THANK YOUR HOMETOWN ANGEL

*We always thank God for all of you, mentioning you
in our prayers. We continually remember before our God
and Father your work produced by faith, your labor
prompted by love, and your endurance inspired by hope
in our Lord Jesus Christ.*

— I THESSALONIANS I:2-3

"Hometown angels" are heroes of the faith right in your own community. They may volunteer in the local homeless shelter or crisis pregnancy center, run a food pantry, lead worship services in a nursing home, or lead after-school programs for underprivileged children. Many of these folks are not paid for their tireless work, yet they do it because they are filled with Christ's love for others. They are the hands and feet of Jesus to those around them.

REACHING IN

You'll need to do a little research in advance for this project. Look up different Christian nonprofit organizations around your community that help others. Write down the address, phone number, and duties of each organization. You can also contact local churches and ask them about members of their congregation who labor with a special ministry.

Take your family to visit each of these places or special people. At each stop, take time to pray for the work done by that organization. If it's open, go inside and greet those working there and learn about their efforts. Ask if you can shoot a video or take photos while touring for a later project. After the tour, return home and discuss the following questions:

For ages 4–7
- Which place do you think helped people the most?
- How would you like to help people?

For ages 8–10
- Can you think of some ways the people we visited showed Jesus' love to others?
- Which of the places we visited would you like to go back to and help out? Why?

For ages 11–13
- How were the people we met today missionaries?
- What kind of missionary work is Jesus calling you to do?

For ages 14 and up
- What inspires these missionaries to do the work they do?
- How have you been inspired to do missionary work?

REACHING INTO THE WORD — MARK 6:30-44

Read the story of the feeding of the 5,000 from Mark 6:30-44, which teaches many great truths, such as we should not overlook the needs of those directly in front of us. Because they didn't want to feed all those hungry people, the disciples suggested that Jesus send them away. Jesus could not do that. He had compassion for the need happening right before His eyes. All we have to do is look around us to find ways to do God's work. The people you visited on your local tour see and respond to those needs every day, just like Jesus. We can all learn from them.

Discuss the following questions together:

- What mistakes did the disciples make in this story?
- How do we sometimes make the same mistakes?

Pray for the hometown angels you met and ask God to help your family show Christ's love to those in need around you.

REACHING INTO THE WORLD

Take the photos or video that you shot on your tour and use them to create a presentation about missions being done in your area. Your presentation can be as high-tech as a PowerPoint presentation or as simple as pictures on poster board. When it's ready, ask a missions group or Sunday school class at your church if you can present it for them. Most groups will jump at the chance for something different like this.

Feel free to make your presentation to other groups as well. The more publicity you can create for these local groups, the better. At the end of your presentation, you can encourage the group to get involved with one of the mission groups or start its own. Finally, pray for God's guidance as you continually look for ways to be Christ in your own community.

TIME OUT . . . IT'S PRAYER TIME

You should pray like this . . .

— MATTHEW 6:9 (CEV)

"The family that prays together stays together." This saying originated in the late 1940s as the motto of Father Patrick Peyton's weekly family radio dramas.[1] Cliché though it may be, it has stuck because of its lasting truth. Families need prayer to survive the stresses and difficulties of life. When a child is teased at school, when a parent loses a job, after a teenager gets his heart broken, or when a loved one dies, families can depend on Christ through prayer.

Individual prayer is very important. A mom prays for her daughter when she studied hard for an exam and didn't do as well as she had hoped. A husband prays for his wife when her mother dies. A sister prays for her brother when he's cut from the basketball team. Prayers such as these strengthen families with a beautiful bond. When we pray for each other and for the world, it brings us closer to God, and we grow in our love for Him. We learn to live a Christ-centered life instead of a self-centered life.

When families pray together, the same thing happens. At dinner and bedtime every evening, we ask our children to take turns praying. Their prayers can range from resistance to routine to rare times of eloquence and real communication. But the regular practice of praying together has taught our children how to normalize prayer in their lives, and it is helping them to love each other, the world, and Christ more.

REACHING IN

Gather at the computer and go to news websites. Look through the headlines for people and situations that need prayer. Print out some of the articles and lay them on the table or floor. Read the stories and discuss how your family can pray for each situation.

Fold the stories up and put them in a bowl. Over the next couple of weeks, at every family meal pull one story out of the bowl and pray about that situation. During the prayer time, give everyone a chance to share their own prayer requests. When it's time to pray, let the children and teens pray. Often, children who wouldn't feel comfortable praying out loud will pray if they can repeat what a parent says. This is a good way to introduce children to praying out loud without having the pressure of trying to think of what to say.

REACHING INTO THE WORD — MATTHEW 6:5-14

Read Matthew 6:5-14. Jesus said this prayer to encourage His disciples about the importance of prayer and to demonstrate different elements of prayer, such as honoring God, crying out for help, requesting forgiveness, forgiving others, and asking to be kept away from sin. Discuss each of these elements and how they relate to what's going on in the lives of your family members today.

Next, select one of the news articles out of the bowl. Take some time to pray for the situation in the article, and then pray for your family. Don't forget to praise God for His goodness and love.

REACHING INTO THE WORLD

Knowing that someone is praying for you is comforting. It helps to know that you're not alone as you deal with sad, frightening, or uncertain times. It shows that others care, even if you've never met them. As your family goes through the bowl of articles and offers up prayers for others, pick a few people you know who are in similar situations that need prayer, and send them a letter. Tell those people that your family is praying for them, and attach a written version of the prayers that were said. Older children and teens can write out a prayer, and small children can draw pictures to show they've been praying for them. In addition, consider keeping in touch with those people and ask them to keep you posted on how your family can continue to pray for them. This will bring overwhelming comfort to the recipients. As for your family, it will build bonds of Christian love that cannot be created in any other way.

8

DIFFERENT, BUT ONE

Honor God by accepting each other,
as Christ has accepted you.

— ROMANS 15:7 (CEV)

Life is full of joy, triumph, pain, and hurt. Families deal with life so much more effectively if they go through it as a united front. When challenges confront a divided family, the fall is long, hard, and destructive. But when a united family faces difficulties, they become stronger and can grow in the love of Christ.

Lasting unity in a family takes daily effort and intentional practice. Every day, teach your family to rally around a member who is having a bad day, to celebrate each other's accomplishments, and to work together to show Christ's love to each other and the world.

REACHING IN

Ask each family member to create an acrostic for the word *unity*. Older children can help younger children if necessary. Very young children can draw pictures of different people getting along and working together. After everyone has finished, allow each person the chance to show his or her creation. Then discuss the following questions:

- How would you rate the unity of our family?
- What are some ways our family can improve its unity?

REACHING INTO THE WORD — ROMANS 15:5-7

Paul wrote these words from a Roman jail. He and his fellow Christ followers knew how crucial it was to stay united in the face of a world that wanted them gone. Paul understood oppression better than anyone, so he wrote these words knowing that his readers would have to heed them in order to survive. Read Romans 15:5-7; then answer the following questions:

For ages 4–7
- When is it hard for you to get along with other family members?
- How does Jesus want us to act toward each other?

For ages 8–10
- The Scripture passage asks us to accept each other. Is that easy or difficult? Explain.
- How does it feel when others accept you?

For ages 11–13
- What do you think it means to be patient and cheerful?
- How can being patient and cheerful benefit the entire family?

For ages 14 and up
- How would you assess your ability to do as the Scripture passage asks?
- How can you be a leader in building family unity and acceptance?

Close this time holding hands in prayer and ask God to make your family unified and to help you find strength in that unity.

REACHING INTO THE WORLD

Not only is it important to be unified as a nuclear family, but it's also crucial for the family of God to be unified. While churches and denominations may have differences in theology, worship styles, and missions emphases, Christians can be unified if we focus on the things we share: our love of Jesus and our place in His family.

Research the missions efforts of other churches in your community. Pick one and volunteer your family to help with one of its missions or outreach programs (for example, another church in town might have a food pantry or clothing drive). You could also enlist the help of other families from your church to make this a larger group effort. This is a great way to strengthen unity among churches.

9

FUTURE FORWARD

God is the one who began this good work in you,
and I am certain that he won't stop before it is complete
on the day that Christ Jesus returns.

— PHILIPPIANS 1:6 (CEV)

It can be frightening not to know what's ahead. The fear you feel when watching a scary movie comes not from what you see but from the anticipation of what you're about to see. It's not so much seeing what's behind the door that gets to us; it's the wondering beforehand about when the door will open and what's going to be behind it.

Fear of the unknown also affects families: Will I get laid off? Is my child's illness something simple or something much worse? How much longer will Grandma be with us? Will my grades be high enough to get that scholarship? What will my life be like after my friend moves away? Waiting for the future to happen can be nerve-racking.

Today's adventure gives your family the opportunity to talk about the future and how you can put it in God's hands.

REACHING IN

Give each person four index cards. Have everyone write down two things they hope *will* happen and two things they hope *won't* happen in the future. Younger children can draw pictures instead. Then have each family member share what's on his or her cards. Discuss the following questions:

- How is the future sometimes exciting and sometimes scary?
- How do you feel about our family's future?

REACHING INTO THE WORD — PHILIPPIANS 1:3-11

Read Philippians 1:3-11. Paul's future seemed bleak. He was in jail with little hope of ever getting out. Yet, he was full of hope because even if he never left his cell, Christ was His savior and would win in the end. Paul was also appreciative of fellow Christians who were working to tell others about Jesus and His love for them.

What can your family learn from Paul's attitude? Here's an exercise that may help you identify some of those things. Take your index cards and, based on the passage, discuss how Paul would have reacted to each situation. Then answer the following questions:

- How can our family lean on each other while waiting for what the future has in store?

- How can we lean on God while waiting for what the future has in store?

When you finish, close your time in prayer and ask God to give you the right attitude about the future. Thank Him for taking care of all of you throughout your lives.

REACHING INTO THE WORLD

Find a local shelter for battered women or another organization that helps women or families in crisis. Here is a way for your family to shine a little light on the situation and offer some hope for their future. Gather infant/toddler supplies such as diapers, formula, baby food, and so on. Create hope boxes for the mothers or families and include things like gift certificates, hand lotion, a Bible, and an invitation to your church, complete with transportation by your family. Your family can gather these items on your own or enlist the help of others, such as church small groups or Sunday school classes. Deliver them as a family to the shelter.

When the project is over, ask God to bless those you've helped by giving them hope and guidance and also to give peace to your family as you face the uncertainties of the future together.

10

ALL OVER THE WORLD

Go to the people of all nations and make them my disciples.
Baptize them in the name of the Father, the Son,
and the Holy Spirit.

— MATTHEW 28:19 (CEV)

There are approximately 57.5 million square miles of land on earth. Before Jesus ascended into heaven, He commanded His followers to spread the Good News to people throughout each and every one of those miles. So how do we accomplish this mission? We do it one person at time, and then one small group at a time.

All of us are missionaries in the sense that we all have been called to fulfill the Great Commission, but God has called some Christians to do so as a vocation. Some minister in churches; others spread the Good News of Jesus to a specific demographic of people. Some missionaries work with inner-city children or youth. Others live and work in a village in Kenya or Chile or the Philippines.

Others may minister to migrant workers. Today's adventure will teach your family about the role of missionaries and how you can help them.

REACHING IN

Collect several magazines and a poster board. Bring your family together and ask each person what he or she thinks a missionary is. Then talk about what it means to be a professional missionary. Search the magazines together and use the poster board to create a collage of images that represents what different missionaries might do.

After you're finished, discuss the following questions:

- What do you think it might be like to be in a family where the parents are missionaries?
- What are some ways our family can support missionaries?

REACHING INTO THE WORD — MATTHEW 28:16-20

Read Matthew 28:16-20, which is known as the Great Commission. In this passage, Jesus gave us the job of helping the whole world learn about Jesus and His love for all of us.

Here's a good way to demonstrate what it means to fulfill the Great Commission. If you have young children, have them help you gather up all their stuffed animals, dolls, and action figures. Then put some in every room. Once all the toys are set, see how quickly your family can go from room to room saying, "Jesus loves you," to every toy.

If your family has teenagers, use a world map to help them

create a list of all the places and people groups in the world where vocational missionaries are needed. Discuss what it must be like to be a missionary in each place.

Once you're finished, read Matthew 28:16-20 again. Then pray for God to bless those who have been called to be missionaries. Ask God to help your family support missionaries you know in every way possible.

REACHING INTO THE WORLD

Find a missionary family through your church's or denomination's missions board. Write a letter to them and include a family photo. Invite the family to share prayer concerns, information about their work, and interesting facts about where they live; ask them to send you a family photo. You could even encourage your kids to become pen pals with their kids. Maintain a regular correspondence with your new friends. Keep their picture on your refrigerator to remind you to always pray for them. Pray for them at family meal times, and perhaps even send cards and notes during holidays since they will be far from relatives during those times.

11

HELPING OTHERS DISCOVER JESUS

The official answered, "How can I understand unless someone helps me?" He then invited Philip to come up and sit beside him.

— ACTS 8:31 (CEV)

It is believed that St. Francis of Assisi once said, "Preach the gospel at all times — if necessary, use words." At its root, missions is the act of helping others discover Jesus and His love for them. We don't even have to speak the name of Jesus to do this. When we prepare a meal for a widow or a family that has lost a loved one, collect canned goods for a food drive, or clean up trash in a local park, we're showing God's love through our actions.

Yet, there comes a time when words are necessary. It can be intimidating to talk about your faith with someone who doesn't share your beliefs. The fear of being rejected or seen as "weird" can keep us from speaking even when we know we should. We think, *Will I say the wrong words and push this person further away from God? Will I come off as insincere and sound like a TV preacher trying to add to his church's numbers?* We fear the timing will be bad and that we will do more harm than good. These fears are valid; most Christians have felt the same discomfort. But when we do what we know we should do—in spite of our fears—those fears will dissipate.

REACHING IN

Hide papers that say "Jesus" around the house. Get blindfolds and gather your family together. Blindfold one member of the family and have him or her go through the house looking for the "Jesus" papers. After a few minutes, the family can start helping that person. Once all the papers have been found, hide them again and repeat the activity with someone else. After everyone has had a turn, answer the following questions:

- What was it like to search for the "Jesus" papers without help?
- How did it feel when others started helping you?
- How is this activity similar to searching for Jesus in life?

REACHING INTO THE WORD — ACTS 8:26-40

One of the many remarkable parts of this story is how God put Philip in just the right place at just the right time to share God's love with the Ethiopian official. God made it clear to Philip what he was to do once he saw the man. God may not usually work this way, but this story is an example of the lengths He will go to to help someone discover His love.

Read the story in Acts 8:26-40. Then answer the following questions:

For ages 4–7

- What must it have felt like for the official to get Philip's help when he couldn't understand the Scriptures?
- When have you needed help understanding the Bible and then got it?

For ages 8–10

- Why do you think the official was so excited after Philip explained the Scripture passage?
- Can you think of a time when you've been excited to learn something about Jesus?

For ages 11–13

- What can we learn from what Philip did in the story?
- Can you think of any friends who need you to be a "Philip" to them?

For ages 14 and up

- Reread verses 32 and 33. How would you have explained the passage to someone who didn't understand it?
- Are you prepared to be a "Philip" every day?

Close your family time in prayer. Ask God to help each of you be a "Philip" to those who are ready and hungry to hear the Good News of Jesus.

REACHING INTO THE WORLD

Identify a nonbelieving family you know, perhaps in your neighborhood or through your children's school. Commit to praying for
them for two weeks. Then make an effort to get to know the family
better and to build a relationship with them. Invite them to dinner
or to a ball game. Let them see your God's love through your family's actions. In time, when you've earned the right to ask, invite
them to join you for church. If they say no, don't be discouraged.
Continue to be their friends and to be there for them. Continue
to pray for them and to build a relationship with them, no matter
what their answer is.

12.

GIVE ME A BREAK!

*The disciple who got there first then went into the tomb,
and when he it, he believed.*

— JOHN 20:8 (CEV)

At one time or another, most of us have felt that we needed a break. Not the kind of break where you rest, although we all need those kinds of breaks too. We're talking about the kind of break where things have been going badly, and you need to have something good happen that's beyond your control and gives you hope.

Easter is that break for all humanity. We look out at the world and see darkness and sin. Then we look at ourselves and find the same things. Death is everywhere, and we know that eventually it will come for us, too. Life seems fleeting and hopeless. Then without warning and without any effort on our part, we catch a break. Jesus, the Son of God, comes to show us ultimate love and sacrifice. He conquers death with His resurrection. He brings us hope for today—and the future—when the odds seemed stacked against us.

REACHING IN

Have everyone look around the house for items you can use to make a cross, and then create one together. Also collect pens, paper, and a stapler. After you've made the cross, have family members think of sins they've committed recently and write them down on paper. (Small children can draw pictures of things they've done wrong.) Next, everyone should fold their paper in half. On the outside, write a prayer asking for forgiveness of those sins on the inside of the paper. (Young children can draw pictures or tell you what to write on the paper.) When everyone is done, staple the papers to the cross.

REACHING INTO THE WORD—JOHN 19–20

Gather some stuffed animals, action figures, and dolls from around the house. Read chapters 19 and 20 in the gospel of John. While you read, have the other family members use the toys as puppets to act out the story. If you only have teenagers, have them close their eyes and visualize the story as it is being read. Then answer the following questions:

- Where in this story is there love?
- How did Jesus give us a break?

Remove the papers from the cross and throw them away. Jesus has erased them! Close in prayer, thanking God for the incredible break He gave us through the cross and Jesus' resurrection.

REACHING INTO THE WORLD

Part of our role as Christians who have been given the ultimate "break" is to look for ways to give other people a break. Your mission is to identify a family in your community that has gone through some hard times and needs to catch a break. Maybe a job was lost or an illness in the family just will not go away, and they've fallen on tough times.

Your family can help by preparing some meals and delivering them to this family. You could offer to do something else to help them as well, such as rake leaves or offer to watch their children during a time when they might need a babysitter. Tell them that your family loves them and that you are keeping their family in prayer. Pray for them daily and ask God to help you be a family that gives others a break.

13

FORGIVENESS HOUSE

If you, O LORD, kept a record of sins, O LORD,
who could stand? But with you there is forgiveness.

— PSALM 130:3-4

In South Africa at the end of apartheid (an oppressive social struc-
ture that made blacks second-class citizens), Archbishop Desmond
Tutu chaired the Truth and Reconciliation Commission. Horrible
atrocities had been committed against his people. The commission
decided not to seek revenge on those who had perpetrated sometimes unspeakable crimes. Instead it chose the way of healing by
granting amnesty in exchange for truth. This kind of justice went a
long way toward bringing healing to a shattered society.[1]

Forgiveness is something we all need but have a hard time
granting to others sometimes. Think about it: Who's hurt you?
Does it still hurt? Have you forgiven that person? In many cases,

we forgive but we don't forget. And often there's a fine line between forgiving and forgetting.

We can also have a hard time forgiving ourselves. The remorseful feelings can be overwhelming, and we can't let go of the bad things we've done.

Forgiveness is a process. We must work hard to give and receive forgiveness. Let's explore what forgiveness means and how it can be fostered in your family.

REACHING IN

As you get ready to make your house a "forgiveness house," gather some poster board, markers, tape, and Bibles. As a family, discuss these questions:

- Think about something that you have done wrong. How did it make you feel?
- What did you do to make it right?
- How do you think God felt when you made that bad choice?
- How do you think God feels when you ask Him for forgiveness and try to make better choices?

Next, discuss ways your family can place a priority on forgiveness. What things would need to change? What behaviors would need to change in order to place greater importance on forgiveness?

Together create a set of rules that foster the practice of forgiveness in your home. (You may want to do the "Reaching Into the Word" activity first, to see what the Bible says about forgiveness, and then come back and create your rules with the Scriptures in mind.) Write five rules on the poster board for your family to follow that will help each member in dealing with forgiveness. For example, you might write, "When someone comes to you to apologize for something he or she has done, talk about your feelings but don't lash out in anger. Remember that everyone needs forgiveness at some point or another." Or, "Always listen to each other, even when you're mad."

Post the rules somewhere in your home to remind your family about your commitment to forgiveness.

REACHING INTO THE WORD — PSALM 130

Psalm 130 is an emotional plea for God's forgiveness. As you read it, you can feel the writer's remorse.

God has given us forgiveness, even though we don't deserve it, because He loves us. He wants us to share that love with others by practicing forgiveness, too. When we forgive others, we are loving them the way Jesus loved us. When our sins separated us from God, Jesus sacrificed His life so we could be reunited with God. That's why forgiveness is so important: It's God's love lived out, here on earth.

Use the following questions as a guide for further discussion.

For ages 4–7
- When have you gotten in trouble for a bad choice?
- How did that make you feel?
- Does God want us to get into trouble or make right choices?

For ages 8–10

- How do you think the writer felt about his sin?
- What was the writer hoping God would do?
- Have you ever had to forgive someone for something? Share some of the details.

For ages 11–13

- According to Psalm 130:3, is anyone *not* a sinner?
- When has forgiveness affected a friendship of yours? Share about that time.

For ages 14 and up:

- Which is harder: to receive forgiveness or to grant it?
- When have you had to ask for forgiveness?
- How do you deal with your feelings when you do something wrong?

Pray together and ask God to help your family make forgiveness part of your daily lives. Thank Him for His mercy, which makes forgiveness possible.

REACHING INTO THE WORLD

Locate the nearest jail, prison, or juvenile detention center. On a weekend morning, go there and stand outside. Housed inside are many people who need forgiveness and who need to offer restitution for what they've done.

Spend some time praying for the inmates inside. Ask God to help them make right choices and live their lives for Jesus. Make contact with the chaplain of that facility and ask for names of inmates to pray for. Commit to pray for them as a family.

If you want to take this to the next level, have each member of your family think of someone whom he or she needs to forgive and pray about the situation. Then write a letter or talk with the person about reconciliation in the relationship.

14

HONKS FROM THE BACK

Therefore encourage one another and build each other up,
just as in fact you are doing.
— I THESSALONIANS 5:11

When geese fly south for the winter, they fly in a V pattern. They honk as they fly together, cheering each other on in their journey to warm weather. That's what our encouragement of one another should look like. As we travel together through life, we should be cheering each other on.

Encouragement is a big gift in a small package. It's easy to give out, and the effects are huge. You can change a life with a few simple words of encouragement.

REACHING IN

Gather some markers and cards, paper, or poster boards.

First, talk about some challenging times you've been through. Listen and ask questions as each person shares. Encourage each other by paying attention to what is said and by speaking positive words or praising the person for doing a good job.

Next, have each person take some markers and something to write on and find a spot by himself or herself. Make encouraging cards, notes, or posters for each person in your family. Afterward, deliver the encouraging messages to each other's rooms.

REACHING INTO THE WORD — 1 THESSALONIANS 5:11

First Thessalonians is a letter to new Christians, encouraging them in the midst of persecution. In this verse, Paul directed the new believers to encourage each other and praised them for already doing so. Paul illustrated what it means to be a powerful encourager.

Paul said to "build each other up," which he demonstrated by telling them to keep up the good work and reminding them to support each other. He knew how vital encouragement is to spiritual health and that it would empower them to keep going. Discuss the following questions:

For ages 4–7
- How does it feel when a friend says something nice to you?
- What should you do when someone is sad?

For ages 8–10

- What does it mean to encourage each other?
- Why is encouragement so important?
- When has someone encouraged you?

For ages 11–13

- What does it mean to build each other up?
- When has someone encouraged you and it made a difference?
- When have you encouraged someone?

For ages 14 and up

- How do you think Paul's encouragement might have helped the new Christians in Thessalonica?
- What are some things our family can do to encourage each other?
- Who do you know that needs some encouragement right now?

Close in prayer and ask God to help your family always look for ways to encourage each other.

REACHING INTO THE WORLD

God gives certain people the gift of encouragement and uses them in important ways in the lives of others. But they need encouragement as well. In this activity, your family is going to encourage an encourager.

Think of someone who encourages others. Buy a journal and arrange for several people to write encouraging notes to that person in the journal. When you have filled up as many pages as you can, present it to that person in appreciation.

15

OUR FIRST JOB

The LORD God took the man and put him in the
Garden of Eden to work it and take care of it.

— GENESIS 2:15

These days we hear a lot about being environmentally friendly. We're encouraged to recycle, conserve energy and water, and use products that don't have adverse effects on the environment. We hear about global warming, tainted water, and polluted air. In fact, we hear about them so much that, at times, we ignore the message to take care of our world.

But God wants us to remember that this is our first job (see Genesis 2:15). He created this amazing world that we live in, and it's our job to preserve this world and all that's in it.

REACHING IN

Have you ever taken a walk outside and wondered how God imagined making everything just the way it is? He crafted thousands upon thousands of flowers that exist in the world today. Both animals and humans rely on the earth for sustenance in a multitude of ways—fruits, vegetables, sunshine, and rain, to name a few. The living creatures that inhabit our world are amazingly unique. God's repertoire of creations is vast and beautiful.

Gather together in a comfortable spot and have everyone close their eyes—except one person, who will read Genesis 1. You've probably heard this passage of Scripture a hundred times already, but this time just listen. With your eyes closed, as that person reads, imagine the earth being formed as you hear it in the story.

When you're finished, share what you thought of as you heard the story, and what amazes you most about God's creation. Is it the many colors God chose for flowers and fruit? Is it the different kinds of fish He made? Is it how He designed nature to feed itself by creating fruit and vegetables and other delicious things that only nature can produce?

If you have younger children, you may want to provide paper and crayons or markers and ask them to draw pictures of the six days of creation and some of the things they are glad God created.

When you think about it, creating something so complex and massive is not something we could ever even aspire to. It displays God's power, creativity, and love.

REACHING INTO THE WORD—GENESIS 1; 2:15

As you've already read, Genesis 1 is all about God creating the earth in six days. It's the beginning of our world, and of us. Though you may be familiar with this story, don't discount the power displayed here. It's beyond any "wow" moment you've ever had in your life.

And after that, right before God created woman, in Genesis 2:15 He told Adam that it was his responsibility to take care of the earth. It's the first job He gave Adam, and we should remember that as Adam's descendents, we are asked to do the same. Discuss the following questions as a family:

For ages 4–7
- What's your favorite part of the Bible story?
- What are you glad that God created?
- How can you help take care of the world?

For ages 8–10
- Name some things that were created in those first six days.
- Why is it so important to God that we take care of the earth?
- What are some things you've done to help take care of the earth?

For ages 11–13
- What does God's creation of the earth and everything in it tell you about Him?
- What are some things you can do to help others see how important it is to take care of the earth?
- What are some things our family can do to take care of the earth?

For ages 14 and up
- What impresses you most about creation?

- What would you like to learn more about in God's creation?
- How can our family get involved on a regular basis in taking better care of the earth?

Pray together and thank God for His beautiful creation. Ask Him to show your family how you can take care of the earth.

REACHING INTO THE WORLD

These days we can take our pick of ways to take care of the environment. There are causes worldwide that are worthy and important. However, for this challenge you have the opportunity to do something for your community.

Find a time one evening or weekend morning to go downtown (or some other area in your community that is well populated). Take trash bags and work gloves for everyone. Find a central location to get started. If your family has the ability to split up, you can do that, or just stay together as you work.

As you walk, look for litter and put it in your trash bag. You can also have separate bags for recyclable material and take them to your local recycling facility when you're done.

When you're finished, wash your hands, take the trash to the appropriate location (dump, recycling center, and so on), and go grab an ice cream together, to celebrate a job well done.

16

SCHOOL'S OUT!

Shout for joy to the LORD, all the earth.

— PSALM 100:1

The word *summer* brings happy thoughts of swimming pools, vacation, amusement parks, and much more. For many kids, the best part of summer is that school and homework are out of sight and out of mind. It's a time to relax, have some fun, and hang out with friends and family.

In the same spirit of kids and summer vacation, Christians should be that joyful every day. We shouldn't be bogged down by burdens and obligations; instead, we should be hopeful and positive, looking forward to the next great thing that God will do. This summer, focus on having fun and being joyful. If your family takes some time to have fun together, you will make memories that will last a lifetime. And you might just show someone else Jesus in the process.

REACHING IN

Schedule an evening for your family to have a "game night" and plan a menu with food that everyone will enjoy. After you've eaten, let everyone choose a game he or she wants to play and play each game together. You could also make these outdoor games, go to the park, or take a walk around the neighborhood. Whatever you decide to do, enjoy just being together as a family.

At the end of the evening, do the "Reaching Into the Word" section together.

REACHING INTO THE WORD — PSALM 100

Psalms are like poems; they convey emotion in a powerful way. Throughout the book of Psalms, the authors express anger, joy, sadness, thanksgiving, and remorse. Psalm 100 explodes with joy and thanksgiving to God. Read Psalm 100 and discuss these questions:

- What's one thing you'll remember about tonight?
- According to verse 5, what can we be joyful about?

End the evening with a prayer, thanking God for the fun you had together and asking Him to help you show the world your joy everywhere you go.

REACHING INTO THE WORLD

Now you can help someone else have joy this summer, too. Set up a lemonade stand on Saturdays in your neighborhood. Instead of keeping the money for yourselves, decide to donate it to your church as a scholarship fund to help cover the cost of camp for a kid whose family may not have the money to send him or her. (If you have older children who don't like the idea of selling lemonade, suggest another way for them to raise money, such as mowing lawns or having a yard sale.)

17

PERFECT DAY

Let the little children come to me, and do not hinder them,
for the kingdom of God belongs to such as these. I tell you
the truth, anyone who will not receive the kingdom of God
like a little child will never enter it.

— MARK 10:14-15

The Bible has several examples of teens and children who have made a difference. David slew Goliath and won a victory for the nation of Israel. Mary gave birth to Jesus, who became the Savior of the world. The boy with the loaves and fish believed that Jesus could do miracles with it—and He did, using it to feed more than five thousand people.

Children and teens can do amazing things for God. From the little girl who begs her parents to take her to church to the teen who uses his own money to go to church camp, kids can and do lead the way for adults when it comes to matters of faith. Our children play a key role in our lives, and God uses them to help accomplish His work in the world.

Let's celebrate the children in our lives by affirming their gifts and all they do for us.

REACHING IN

Take a moment to ask your children their idea of a perfect day. No holds barred, no limits on time or money or parental guidance. Invite them to share all of their ideas, and listen to them. What do you hear them saying? They might say they'd skip school, order pizza for breakfast, play video games, invite their friends over for ice cream, go to the candy store, go shopping, go swimming, or maybe just have authority over the remote control all day. Perhaps they'd say that you would take off work and take them to the park. Or maybe they would choose to sleep in and then spend the afternoon playing basketball with friends. Listen to their wishes and see if you can detect some of their secret desires or even their needs.

Next, get some paper and pencils (for younger children, get markers or crayons, too). Together, plan out a perfect day that your family can enjoy together. Get input from everyone and include at least one thing that each person wants to do. Create a schedule. As you plan, keep in mind that this is something you will actually do. Have younger children decorate the schedule with pictures of the ideas your family has come up with.

Finally, schedule a time to spend your perfect day together. As you enjoy your day, think about the contribution your children make to your family. Be sure to praise them for who they are, what they can do, and how God has given them special gifts.

REACHING INTO THE WORD — MARK 10:13-16

This Scripture passage is well-known and well-loved. It demonstrates how we should respond to God's gift of salvation — that we should receive it with the trust and belief of a child. We can't earn God's love; we can only accept it, because it is God's gift to us. Read the passage and then discuss the following questions:

For ages 4–7
- What does Jesus think about children?
- How can kids help others know about Jesus?
- What do you hope people learn about Jesus?

For ages 8–10
- Why did Jesus correct the disciples?
- What does Jesus think children can help others do?
- How can we help others know more about Jesus?

For ages 11–13
- How does it make you feel to know that Jesus puts great importance on children?
- What are some gifts you can use to help others know about Jesus?
- Why is it important to celebrate children?

For ages 14 and up
- What lesson has a child taught you or helped you to understand?
- How would you praise the children in your life for their influence on you?

- How can you empower the children in your life to participate in God's work right now?

Pray together and thank God for the ways that your children
teach you about God. Ask Him to take care of them and guide
them.

REACHING INTO THE WORLD

The focus of this activity is all about celebrating children. Jesus said
that we must receive the kingdom of God like a child; otherwise,
we'll never enter it. It's good to recognize the lessons God can teach
us through our children and to celebrate their gifts and contribu-
tions to our family and, on a larger scale, the body of Christ.

Plan to make gift bags for all the kids in your neighborhood.
Visit a local fast-food restaurant or favorite place of kids in your
community, and ask if they'll be willing to donate (or sell to you at
a discounted price) coupons for free kid's meals. Explain that you'll
be passing them out to children in the community who might be
looking for a church home. If donations or discounts aren't an
option, you could also see if people at your church would be willing
to donate money to buy coupons or gift cards.

Next, assemble gift bags. This could be a multifamily effort or
even a churchwide effort. Include the coupons, a card from your
church that shows its meeting times and children's activities, and
anything else kids would like that is economical to buy in bulk.

On a Saturday or Sunday afternoon, walk to the houses in
your neighborhood and offer the gift bags to all the kids (with their
parents' permission).

Another idea is to assemble and pass out the gift bags to kids in your church, with enough for guests. Ask the kids to invite any friends who don't already go to church. Make sure they tell their friends that anyone who comes to church gets a gift bag. After the service, pass out the gift bags to all the kids.

18

BANK ON IT

*I am going to make a solemn promise to you and
to everyone who will live after you.*

— GENESIS 9:9 (CEV)

People renege on their promises all the time. The salesman says that the price won't go any lower. Your boss commits to a raise next year. The politician says he will fix the potholes in the road. Each time someone fails to deliver on a promise, our trust in humanity is shaken just a little bit more.

Broken promises can be infinitely more damaging when those close to us break their word. The mother who promises to play a game with her son but doesn't follow through; the husband who breaks a wedding vow; the child who doesn't study after promising to do better—all whittle away at the foundation of trust necessary for a strong and loving family. Some of us have been crushed by so many broken promises that trust is now close to impossible.

Oftentimes we continually break promises to ourselves, causing a distrust and loathing even of self.

God makes promises as well. He promises to love us, take care of us, and even save us. Sometimes it seems as though He, too, has failed to keep His vows, causing a crushing hurt beyond words. When it seems that even our Creator has abandoned us, darkness can overwhelm. But despite how we may feel, God will never abandon us or break His promises to us. Even when everyone else has failed us, He stands firm in His love and support. We may not feel it or believe it at times, but He is there.

Today your family will learn about God's promises to us, and you will get the opportunity to make a promise to someone who really needs some help and to follow through on that promise.

REACHING IN

Get a piece of poster board and a marker and draw a line down the middle. Ask everyone to think of a promise that someone made to them. On one side of the line, have everyone write that promise; on the other side of the line, write how it turned out (if the promise was kept or not). Small children could draw pictures.

When you're finished, discuss the following questions:

For ages 4–7
- How does it feel when someone breaks his or her promise to you?
- What promises does God make?

For ages 8–10
- How does a broken promise hurt a friendship?
- Can we rely on God's promises? Why?

For ages 11–13
- What are some promises that you can do a better job of keeping?
- Why do we sometimes mistrust God's promises?

For ages 14 and up
- How has the totality of kept and broken promises in your life changed you?
- How can choosing to trust in God's promises change you?

REACHING INTO THE WORD — GENESIS 9:8-17

Read Genesis 9:8-17, where God made a solemn promise to Noah and every living creature that He would never again destroy the earth with a flood. Then He put His seal on the promise via a rainbow. Get out some paper and markers and draw several rainbows. Under each rainbow, write out a promise that God has made to you and how He has fulfilled that promise. Then close in prayer, asking God to help all of us keep our promises and have faith that He will keep His promises as well.

REACHING INTO THE WORLD

Think of a person in your church, work, or neighborhood who has been hurt by broken promises — perhaps an adult who has been divorced or a child in a broken home. Contact that person and tell him or her that your family is going to commit to pray for him or her over the next month, making a promise to do that. Ask for specific ways your family can pray.

Then over the next four weeks, pray for that person on a regular basis. Every week, send a note or e-mail reminding him or her that your family is praying. Your family will be restoring at least a little bit of the trust in humanity that the person lost, and your children will learn the importance of keeping a promise.

19

DOWNTIME

*By the seventh day God had finished the work he had been
doing; so on the seventh day he rested from all his work.
And God blessed the seventh day and made it holy, because
on it he rested from all the work of creating
that he had done.*

— GENESIS 2:2-3

In 1965, seventeen-year-old Randy Gardner stayed up for more
than eleven straight days. It was considered a world record at the
time. During his experiment he began to hallucinate, became para-
noid, and experienced short-term memory loss.[1]

While his ability to stay up for eleven days is impressive, it also
shows what can happen to us when we don't get the rest we need.
We often underestimate the importance of rest in our lives. We're
so focused on what we can get done that we often forget about the
benefits of good rest. It helps our bodies recharge and heal from all

the activity of life. Without rest, we could do damage to our bodies and minds. Everyone needs that downtime.

God set the example for us. After creating the world in six days, He took a day to rest and called it holy. We honor that day by going to church, worshipping with our church family, taking time to reflect on what God has been doing in us, and preparing for what He will do in the week to come. A time of resting from our work can rejuvenate and recharge us. It can also be a time to focus on something other than our jobs, schedules, and the daily grind of life.

REACHING IN

Find a comfortable spot to sit together, maybe under a tree in your backyard, on your deck, or at a restaurant during dinner. Share times you can remember when you got a really good rest. Maybe it was a vacation, a day off from work or school, or an evening alone curled up with a good book.

Next, share about some things you need rest from right now. Maybe you've been working a lot and you just need a break. Maybe you're about to finish a big project and you're hoping things will slow down once it's finished.

Next, share about someone you know who could use a rest. What's been going on in his or her life lately? Why hasn't that person been able to get the downtime he or she needs? For the "Reaching Into the World" activity, you'll do something special for one of those people you mentioned, so pray and ask God to help you as you plan this.

REACHING INTO THE WORD — GENESIS 2:1-3

This Scripture passage shows what is probably a rare moment for God—He rested. The creation of the world and everything in it probably took a lot out of Him. He was very pleased with the work He'd done, so He took a break afterward. He used it as a lesson for us—that we should make time to rest, too.

As you read the verses and answer the questions below, think about what God wants you to learn from His example of why we should take time to rest.

For ages 4–7

- When is your time to rest?
- Why should we all rest?
- How does it help us when we rest?

For ages 8–10

- According to the Scripture, what did God do on the seventh day?
- When have you enjoyed a rest after hard work?
- How does rest help us? Why is it better for others when we rest?

For ages 11–13

- Does it surprise you that God rested? Why or why not?
- Why do you think God wants us to know He rested?
- How can our rest time be helpful to others as well?

For ages 14 and up

- When has a time of rest improved an area of your life?

- What's one thing you've done during a rest time that benefited someone else?
- How can you make changes in your life to include more rest time?

Close in prayer, thanking God for the times of rest and rejuvenation that your family has enjoyed together. Ask Him to show you someone else you can help to get some rest as well.

REACHING INTO THE WORLD

Identify one of the people you mentioned during the "Reaching In" activity who could use a rest. What are some things you could do for that individual to provide a way for him or her to rest? For example, if you know a single parent, perhaps you could offer to babysit or take care of errands or housework to help lighten the load.

20

YOU'RE NEVER OUT

You were saved by faith in God, who treats us
much better than we deserve. This is God's gift to you, and
not anything you have done on your own.
— EPHESIANS 2:8 (CEV)

In his book *What's So Amazing About Grace?* author Philip Yancey told a story about a British conference on comparative religions. A group of scholars were gathered together, debating whether Christianity has any attribute unique to itself. They began eliminating possibilities. Other religions have an incarnation and resurrection story. They advocate the same moral teachings. The debate went on for some time until the great Christian scholar C. S. Lewis walked into the room. He asked, "What's the rumpus about?" After they explained to him the nature of the debated issue, he said, "Oh, that's easy. It's grace." After more discussion, everyone agreed. All other religions offer different ways to earn God's favor; only

Christianity offers us God's unconditional love through grace.[1]

God's offer of grace proves His perfect love for each and every one of us. Once we've received this love, it's our responsibility to show the same grace-filled love to others.

REACHING IN

Gather your family together for a game of Simon Says, where one person makes the others do what he or she instructs by calling out, "Simon says . . ." (pat your head, stomp your feet, and so on). Anyone who doesn't follow the directions is out of the game. Eventually the leader will try to trick the others by giving a command without saying, "Simon says," first. Those who follow the command are out.

Give every member of the family a chance to be Simon. You will go last. As you play Simon, don't make anyone sit out for messing up. Keep giving everyone chance after chance. When the game is over, debrief by discussing the following questions:

- How was the game different for you when Simon didn't make you sit out when you messed up?
- Which version of Simon Says is most like life? The one where you don't get put out for mistakes or the one where you do? How so?
- Which version is God's way like? Explain.

REACHING INTO THE WORD — EPHESIANS 2:8-10

Look up Ephesians 2:8-10 and read it to your family. Paul understood the key Christian principle of grace as well as any Christian in history. When his name was Saul, he opposed the way of Christ to the point of leading the charge to prosecute and sometimes even execute those who were followers of Jesus. That was until one day when he was confronted by the grace of God. Afterward he changed his name to Paul and preached the Good News of Jesus all over the known world. Even though Paul had spent a lifetime trying to destroy Christianity, God gave him grace and saw what he could become. So, when Paul wrote these words, he intimately realized the importance of grace.

Discuss the passage using the following questions:

For ages 4–7

- When someone is mean to you, what is the first thing you want to do back?
- What do you think Jesus would want you to do?

For ages 8–10

- Is it hard to forgive those who try to hurt you?
- How often does God forgive us?

For ages 11–13

- Is it more natural to forgive or seek revenge?
- What does God's grace feel like?

For ages 14 and up

- What does a lack of grace on others do to your soul?
- What does it mean to fully accept grace?

Close your time together in prayer. Ask God to teach your family to have grace on each other and everyone else. Praise God for His grace on all of us, which demonstrates His perfect love.

REACHING INTO THE WORLD

On a hot day, pack a cooler full of bottled water and/or other drinks. Go to the park and give the drinks to those who neglected to bring a beverage and could really use some hydration. If some ask why you're offering free drinks, just say that your family wanted to help out people who needed something to drink on a hot day. If the conversation goes further, you may find an opening to tell them that your family is trying to emulate God's love and grace.

This small act of kindness will offer others a glimpse into the grace and love of God. On your way home, take time to pray for each individual you met and helped out.

21

CHURCH IN THE SPOTLIGHT

In a powerful way the apostles told everyone that the Lord
Jesus was now alive. God greatly blessed his followers.

— ACTS 4:33 (CEV)

In the 1960s Simon and Garfunkel's famous hit song "I Am a
Rock" was about a person trying to live life alone without the risk
of companionship. Do you sense the deep hurt in the following
line: "I have no need of friendship; friendship causes pain"?

For some, this attitude stems from a bad experience with a
church. These folks build walls and don't go back to any church so
that they can protect themselves from future hurts. When you've
been hurt, it's hard to remember that churches are full of deeply
flawed people, just like the rest of the world.

Yet God gave us the gift of the church because the

alternative — not having a community of people to "do life" with — is so much more difficult. We were never meant to live out our Christian life alone, without the family of God to lean on. Yes, we may risk some hurt along the way, but we need the support and encouragement of fellow Christ followers.

REACHING IN

Using one hundred index cards and a pen, have your family write down as many people, events, and situations you can think of that your church provides that benefit your family. Everything you can think of counts — from your Sunday school teacher to the nursery workers to the fall festival to the sound-booth technicians. Try your best to use all one hundred cards.

When you're done, pick a room in your house where you can spread out all of the cards. Pray together, thanking God for your church and how the people and services offered have helped your family grow spiritually.

REACHING INTO THE WORD — ACTS 2:42-47

Today millions upon millions of people consider themselves to be Christians. At the time that this Scripture passage was written, the number of believers was likely in the hundreds, and powerful entities all around them were looking for their demise. In order to survive, these early Christians knew the only way to grow and thrive was to lean on each other for everything. We can learn much from the tight-knit community that they formed. Read Acts 2:42-47 and use the following questions to facilitate a discussion about church.

For ages 4–7
- What are some of your favorite things about going to church?
- Why does God want us to go to church?

For ages 8–10
- How does church help us follow Jesus?
- How can we help make the church what God wants it to be?

For ages 11–13
- How can church help you through tough times?
- How can we help our friends find the help they need at church?

For ages 14 and up
- Why does the church sometimes fail people?
- How can you be part of making sure it doesn't fail people?

Close your time of discussion in prayer. Ask God to reveal ways each person in your family can help make your church a more loving and caring place. Ask God to help your family lean on the church community for growth, friendship, and love. Lastly, thank God for your church family.

REACHING INTO THE WORLD

Part of the church's role is to welcome outsiders. Not only is the church is to love and be an anchor for people within its walls, it's also to serve as a beacon of light to people who have not yet connected to the family of God.

Offer your family as a contact for new families or people in your church who are interested in a small group. When your church staff learns of a family's interest, they would let you know. Your family could invite them to breakfast or to your house for dessert as a way to get to know them better and help them find the right place to get plugged in. Familiarize yourself with all the groups your church has available so you can share the options with them.

Remember to pray for the people before and after you talk with them, asking God to help them become more connected in your church family.

22

NEW BEGINNINGS

Because of the LORD's great love we are not consumed,
for his compassions never fail. They are new every morning;
great is your faithfulness.

— LAMENTATIONS 3:22-23

In 1908 the Chicago Cubs won the World Series. As of the writing of this book, they haven't won it since. Yet every April on opening day, Wrigley Field is sold out, with fans believing it's a new beginning. "This year is the year," you'll hear them say.

Everyone deserves a fresh start, just as the Cubs get one every April. The chance to begin again is central to what we believe as Christians. Jesus paid it all with His life so we could have another chance.

REACHING IN

Find a place in your home where your kids can be hams as though they were on a stage. If you've got younger children who like to draw, you could have them create pictures for this activity instead.

Ask your kids to daydream about what they hope the next six months will be like. Maybe they have hopes of being the lead in the school play, learning the saxophone, running track, learning to write with cursive letters, or making the honor roll.

Next, have them create a skit (or play a game of Charades) about their dreams. Again, younger kids could draw pictures instead.

Finally, have them think of ideas for what they can do to work toward their goal. On paper, help your kids create a plan for accomplishing one of their dreams. When you finish, put the lists someplace where you can refer back to them on a regular basis in order to help your kids remember their dream and their plan for making it a reality.

REACHING INTO THE WORD — LAMENTATIONS 3:22-23

God's faithfulness is great, and His kindness and love are "new every morning." Because of God's love, we can have a new start. Whatever disappointments we may have had in the past can be put aside; with lessons learned and new motivation, we can try to attain new goals. Read the verses and then discuss the following questions:

For ages 4–7
- What's coming up soon that you're excited about?

- What are some things you'd like to do in the coming weeks?
- How can God help you with those things you want to do?

For ages 8–10

- How do you think a new day might be like a "do-over"?
- How does it feel to know you can make a fresh start?
- What do you hope happens in the coming weeks? What do you hope doesn't happen?

For ages 11–13

- The Scripture says God's compassion is "new every morning." What do you think that means?
- According to verse 22, what keeps us from being consumed? What do you think the writer meant by *consumed*?
- How might knowing that God is faithful help you with the future?

For ages 14 and up

- When have you felt consumed by a challenging experience or a disappointment?
- When has God given you a chance to start over? Share about that time.
- How does it make you feel to know that God's compassion is new every morning?

Close in prayer, thanking God for His daily compassions and the fresh start He gives us whenever we need it.

REACHING INTO THE WORLD

The beginning of a new school year would be a great time to do this activity. However, this can be done any time of the year because school supplies are always needed.

Think about those families who struggle with the expense of school supplies. How can you help? You might contact your school and ask if you could donate supplies for someone who might need them. Find out what you need to buy, and go shopping as a family! Your kids will know better than you what their fellow students will appreciate, so make sure you include them when selecting the supplies.

23

LEAD ON

And if your Lord and teacher has washed your feet,
you should do the same for each other.

— JOHN 13:14 (CEV)

Leadership can be modeled in all sorts of ways. There's the field marshal, directing others with sure and strong commands. There are those who lead by example, showing everyone the way through their actions. Then there's the team builder, who builds consensus within the group and then acts on the decisions made.

While all of these leaders have their place, the Bible emphasizes one special kind of leader called the servant leader. Jesus demonstrated this revolutionary kind of leadership through His words, deeds, and ultimately through the cross. Servant leadership requires fearless self-sacrifice; it means putting others before yourself, and sacrificing your own needs for others.

When the family of God becomes servant leaders, the change is breathtaking. When everyone begins to lead by serving, the atmosphere that once may have been selfish, political, and petty becomes loving and caring. When leadership is servant-based, God's family can begin to show the world the true nature of Christ's love.

The same is true of every family. Servant leadership makes our homes the loving and giving places God means for them to be.

REACHING IN

Gather your family to explain the ground rules for a weeklong challenge. Each person is to be a servant leader by doing each other's chores and taking care of each other's needs in as many ways as possible, without having to be told. For example, if taking out the trash is your husband's responsibility, take care of it before he can get to it. If your sister's room could use some straightening up, do it while she's watching TV. If your mom looks worn out from a hard day, fix her something to drink. Each family member should keep track of what he or she has accomplished. Very young children may need some direction and help through the week, but don't underestimate their ability to participate.

At the end of the week, get together and discuss what happened along with the following questions:

- How did it feel to serve others in our family?
- What was it like when a family member served you?
- How would behaving like this all the time change our family?
- Why does Jesus want us to lead in this way?

REACHING INTO THE WORD — JOHN 13:1-17

Turn to John 13:1-17 and read the passage as a family. Jesus wanted to teach His disciples the importance of servant leadership; by washing their feet, He engraved the lesson on their minds for life. The Messiah stooped down to serve those He led.

Using a bucket and a washcloth, take some time to wash each other's feet just as Jesus did in the story. After you're done, discuss servant leadership further, using the following questions:

- Why do you think Jesus emphasized servant leadership over other types of leadership?
- How does God want us to lead by serving our friends, church, and world?
- When is it hardest to be a servant leader?

Close with prayer, asking God to teach your family to lead each other and the world through servanthood.

REACHING INTO THE WORLD

Think of some people in your neighborhood who need help with their homes. Maybe they need their lawns mowed, leaves raked, or snow shoveled. Organize your family to lead through service. Ask those people if your family can come by and take care of one or more of their needs. Then load up the car with whatever equipment you need and go serve. When you're done, pray for the people you have helped.

24

STAYING CONNECTED

I am the vine, and you are the branches. If you stay joined
to me, and I stay joined to you, then you will produce lots of
fruit. But you cannot do anything without me.
— JOHN 15:5 (CEV)

Our two most basic physical needs are food and water. Without food and water, a person will die within three to five days. That's all it takes to be cut off from nutrients before we die. The love of Christ is the critical nutrient for our souls. Being cut off from Him starves the soul and eventually leads to spiritual death.

John 15 paints a perfect picture of what it means to connect with Jesus and produce "fruit." When Jesus said *fruit,* He was referring to spreading His love to others. Ultimate love comes from Jesus, and when we are connected to His "vine," His love fills us and overflows to others. We want to use our gifts and talents to partner with God in redeeming the world and the people whom He created.

REACHING IN

Gather your family in the kitchen. It's time to make the ultimate fruit salad with every fruit you have in the kitchen or pantry. Make certain everyone gets a chance to help create this tasty treat. When you're done, give everyone a bowl of fruit, topped with some sugar or whipped cream if you want.

While you're eating, discuss this question: "What fruit are you most like and why?" When you're done, put the rest of the fruit salad in the refrigerator because you'll need it later.

Explain to your family that branches that stay connected to the vine bear fruit. In the same way, when we stay connected to Jesus, who is our vine, our lives can bear fruit, too.

REACHING INTO THE WORD — JOHN 15:1-17

Read John 15:1-17. Give everyone paper and markers to draw a vine and branches while you read the passage. Or have your family gather outside by a tree while you read. After you finish reading, discuss the Scripture passage using the following questions as a guide.

For ages 4–7
- What do branches need to stay alive?
- What special abilities has God given you to help others?

For ages 8–10
- How are our lives like the branches Jesus talks about?
- What does Jesus mean by producing fruit, and how can you produce some?

For ages 11–13

- Why do we sometimes want to break away from Jesus?
- When is it hard to bear fruit? Why?

For ages 14 and up

- If the vine brings life, why do so many reject it?
- What fruit do you sense God wanting you to produce that you don't produce now?

Close in prayer, asking God to give your family the nourishment it needs to produce beautiful and healthy fruit.

REACHING INTO THE WORLD

Think of someone in your church or community who has been like a branch and stayed connected to Jesus and shared His love with others over the years. Take the rest of your fruit salad to that person. Tell the person that your family has been studying John 15 and that the passage caused you to think of him or her. Thank the person for being an inspiration to your family and let him or her know that your family hopes to spend many years bearing fruit. Pray for the person before you leave and thank God for his or her years of fruitful service to Him.

WE GOT GIFTS!

Just as each of us has one body with many members, and
these members do not all have the same function,
so in Christ we who are many form one body, and
each member belongs to all the others. We have different
gifts, according to the grace given us.

— ROMANS 12:4-6

Gifts are often thought of as boxes wrapped in pretty paper and presented to a loved one, items selected after careful thought and time spent choosing what is "just right" for the recipient.

But gifts don't have to be tangible. They can be special abilities. *The Guinness Book of World Records* chronicles many special feats. For example, the heaviest weight dangled from a swallowed sword? Fifty-five pounds, one ounce. Fastest time to pluck a turkey? One minute, thirty seconds. These are impressive skills![1]

God gives each of us what the Bible calls "spiritual gifts," or special skills He chose carefully for each one of His children. Our gifts serve a purpose in God's plan that we be salt and light in the world.

REACHING IN

Gather together with paper, markers, and gift boxes. First, have family members identify some favorite gifts they've received over the years. These gifts could be nice things or loving actions. Next, together consider all the members in your family and what special skills they have that you feel God has given them. Make a list for each person of everyone's ideas about his or her skills.

Then give the following directions to everyone: Take paper, markers, and a gift box for each person in the family (except yourself). Find a place where you can spend a few minutes alone to think about each person. Write each person's name at the top of a piece of paper, then write (or draw a picture of) one skill or ability that you feel that person has and explain why. When you finish, put each paper in a gift box and write the person's name on top of the box.

Take ten minutes to do this; then come back together. Pass out the gifts and take time to watch each person open his or her gifts and show what's inside.

Finally, ask if anyone has questions about how to use his or her skills for God. Brainstorming together can help strengthen your family bond and show your kids that what we do in life has an eternal impact. As you brainstorm, write your ideas on the lists you created for each person earlier. They can keep their lists to remind themselves of how gifted they are.

REACHING INTO THE WORD — ROMANS 12:4-8; 1 PETER 4:10

In Romans 12:4-8, Paul compared God's followers to a body, and everyone is a different part of that body. The parts working together make the whole body function. It's a great example of how we should work together as Christians and recognize that everyone's gifts are important to the overall health of the body. In 1 Peter 4:10, we are encouraged to use whatever gifts we have for God so that He is honored in everything we do.

As you read the Scriptures together and discuss the following questions, consider how your gifts fill a role in the body of Christ, as well as how your family's gifts can work together to honor God.

For ages 4–7
- What do you think you're good at?
- How could you use those gifts to do good things for God?
- What's one thing you can do this week with your special gift?

For ages 8–10
- In Romans 12:4-5, what is the body Paul talked about?
- What does God want us to do with our gifts?
- How are you going to use your gifts?

For ages 11–13
- How does it feel to know that, as a follower of God, you're part of a body of people that works together?
- How did it feel to hear what your family members believe your gifts are?

- Were there some gifts you didn't know you had? Share about them.
- How do you feel God is leading you to use those gifts?

For ages 14 and up
- What are some of the gifts mentioned in the Scripture passage in Romans?
- No matter what our gifts are, what should they always do? (See 1 Peter 4:10.)
- What are some ways you currently use your gifts? What are some new ways you can use them?

Pray together and thank God for your gifts. If there are some in your family who don't know what their gifts are, ask God to show them.

REACHING INTO THE WORLD

How could you use your gifts to help others around you? Take time to brainstorm some people who might need extra help or encouragement and how your gifts could help them. Choose one person you can help by doing something that uses a gift from every member of your family.

For example, you might know an elderly woman who lives alone. Your family could visit with her, take her dinner, your kids could draw her pictures or sing a few of her favorite songs with her, read the Bible to her, take care of odd jobs around her house, and so on. Think of things to do that would help her and utilize the gifts of each family member. As you do, you'll be fulfilling God's purposes for the gifts He's given you.

26

BEAUTIFUL WORDS

The Scriptures train God's servants to do all kinds
of good deeds.
— 2 TIMOTHY 3:17 (CEV)

Martin Luther is best known as the leader of the Protestant Reformation, but he did something that is an even greater contribution to Christianity. In a time when the standard language of the Bible was Latin, and the idea of translating it into any modern language was unthinkable, Luther decided to translate the Bible into his native German. The outcome shook the world. People who had never read the Bible before could now read it for themselves, and they didn't have to rely on a priest to tell them what it meant. They experienced for themselves the power of God's Holy Word.

Today, more copies of the Bible have been printed, and in more languages, than any other book in history. No other book has been as closely studied, scrutinized, and debated by people of all backgrounds. We can study the Scriptures for ourselves and experience the history, poetry, stories, and letters that teach us God's truth.

Every time we open the Bible, God can teach us something new. Every time we think we understand, it whisks us off on another wild and unpredictable journey. The humbling adventure of studying the Bible never ends.

REACHING IN

Get some index cards, pens, and markers, and then call your family together. Tell them that today you're going to celebrate God's gift of the Bible. Give everyone five index cards and ask them to write on each index card a favorite passage or story from the Bible. Small children can draw pictures of their favorite Bible stories. If you really want to go all out, plan a family party with good food and games along with the activity.

Once everyone has finished, give each family member a couple of minutes to hide his or her index cards somewhere in the house. Then search for everyone else's index cards. After your family finds all the cards, have each person read out loud the cards he or she found and try to guess who chose that verse as a favorite passage. Then have the person who chose the passage explain how that Scripture has encouraged or helped him or her.

REACHING INTO THE WORD — 2 TIMOTHY 3:16-17

Turn to 2 Timothy 3:16-17 and read it aloud. Paul's letter to his young protégé, Timothy, and the church Timothy served, gives advice on many church issues, including the importance of studying Scripture and using it as a life guide. Use the following questions to help you discuss the importance of Scripture.

For ages 4–7
- Why do we read the Bible?
- What does the Bible teach you?

For ages 8–10
- What are some of your favorite lessons from the Bible?
- How can it be useful to you every day?

For ages 11–13
- How can you make the Bible part of your daily life?
- What kinds of situations can it help you through?

For ages 14 and up
- What parts of the Bible do you need to study more closely?
- What plan can you make to learn more about those parts of the Bible?

Close your time together in prayer, asking God to guide you as your family uses the Bible to grow and learn.

REACHING INTO THE WORLD

Go to your local Christian bookstore or an Internet site and purchase a few copies of the Bible. Deliver them to people in your church or community who could use one. Perhaps a child attends your church alone, with no family support, and doesn't own a Bible at all. Maybe you know an elderly person who could use the Bible on audio because his or her eyesight has grown poor. (There are many websites that have the Bible available for download at a reasonable price; www.freechristianaudiobooks.com is one.) It might also be fun if your family members shared their favorite Bible stories with this person as well as what the Bible has meant to your family. After you've delivered the Bibles, pray as a family for the individuals you helped. Ask God to use the Bibles to connect them with His truth and love.

27

BUSTING INJUSTICE

Moses answered the people, "Do not be afraid. Stand firm and you will see the deliverance the LORD will bring you today. The Egyptians you see today you will never see again. The LORD will fight for you; you need only to be still."

— EXODUS 14:13-14

In the spring of 1963, the Reverend Martin Luther King Jr. and other civil rights leaders led a protest in what was then segregated Birmingham, Alabama. City officials squashed the peaceful demonstration with high-pressure water hoses and dogs. King was arrested. The horrible images were broadcast all over the world and greatly strengthened support for desegregation. King relied on his faith in Jesus while facing down powerful injustice.

What do you do when you see injustice? Draw attention to it? Walk away from it? Pray about it? Try to fix the situation? There are many different responses to unfair situations. Injustice is everywhere, and it demands a response. What's yours?

REACHING IN

Sit down with your family in a circle in your backyard or in a park and pass out an uninflated balloon to each person. Take a few minutes to identify some of the injustices your family sees in the world, your community, your school, and anywhere else you can think of. Have each person share one injustice and then blow up his or her balloon. Once everyone has shared, put all the balloons in the middle of the circle.

Now stand up, but stay in your circle. For each injustice you thought of, think of ways you could take a stand for others in those situations. For each idea, pop a balloon by stomping on it. Do this until all the balloons are popped.

REACHING INTO THE WORD — EXODUS 14:13-14

At the end of Exodus 13, Moses led the Israelites out of Egypt. In this passage, just a few verses later, Pharaoh and his army were chasing after them. Moses and his people were trapped between Pharaoh's army and the Red Sea. Moses showed his leadership in these verses by assuring the people that God would make a way and help them escape from the injustice that Egypt had put upon them for centuries. The miracle that happened next was the parting of the Red Sea.

These verses are encouraging and comforting, but if you read closely, you can sense empowerment in them, too. To hear that "the LORD will fight for you" is like a power surge that has the potential to squash our fears and help us stand up against injustice.

As you read the verses and answer the questions below, think about how you can take a stand for those who are treated unjustly and how your family can pray that God would fight for those who cannot fight for themselves.

For ages 4–7

- When have you said, "That's not fair"? Describe what happened.
- How can we help someone who is sad because he or she was treated badly?
- How does it make you feel to know that God will help those who are treated badly?

For ages 8–10

- In verse 13, Moses told the people to stand firm. What do you think that means?
- What are some examples of standing firm?
- When has someone helped you when you were treated unfairly?

For ages 11–13

- In verse 13, Moses told the people not to be afraid. What is scary about standing up for the injustice we see?
- When have you been involved in unjust treatment?
- What unfair situation do you see going on right now that you wish you could do something about?

For ages 14 and up

- If you had been with the people Moses was addressing and had heard his words, how would it have made you feel?
- Who do you know that needs God to fight for him or her?

- What's one thing your family can do to help bust injustice in your area?

Close in prayer and ask God to help you see and stand up for injustice.

REACHING INTO THE WORLD

Sometimes we pay more attention to what's happening on the other side of the world than to what's going on in our own communities. What are some organizations that fight injustice in your community? Maybe a local mission or nonprofit organization, a church reaching out to people in need, or a group that provides a service to the community? Find a place locally that could use some public support or attention.

First, go visit the place as a family and talk with the people. Find out what they do and maybe spend some time shadowing them as they perform their tasks.

Next, write a letter to the editor of your local newspaper to show support for that organization. Describe what the organization does and what it contributes to your city. This show of public support makes others aware of how they can be of help.

You could also take the information back to your church and encourage others to get involved with helping that organization fight injustice in your community.

28

PUSHING THROUGH

*God will bless you, if you don't give up when your faith is
being tested. He will reward you with a glorious life,
just as he rewards everyone who loves him.*

— JAMES 1:12 (CEV)

It's not a matter of *if* life will throw a difficult challenge at us, it's
a matter of *when*. Sometimes we face small challenges, such as a
sinus infection or a car repair. Other times the challenges become
more serious, like when a teenage daughter announces her pregnancy or a husband needs help for depression. Then there are those
catastrophic challenges that almost destroy us, such as the death of
a loved one or a divorce.

How will we handle it, and who will we lean on as we persevere through the troubles? Family and friends are terrific options.
However, the more grounded we are in Jesus, the stronger we will
be in the face of life's greater challenges, and the more peace we will
experience as we push through them.

REACHING IN

Have the family search their closets for the oldest, grubbiest pairs of shoes they can find. Then take turns talking about the shoes and what you did to get them to their current condition. After everyone has had a turn, discuss the following questions:

- Think of some difficult times you've been through. How have they worn you down?
- Who or what helped you push through the situation?
- How can you help each other deal with life's challenges?
- What does it mean to persevere? Why do you think it's an important character quality?

REACHING INTO THE WORD — JAMES 1:2-4,12

Take a look at James 1 verses 2-4 and 12. In some ways James can be seen as a New Testament book of wisdom (a little like Proverbs in the Old Testament). This letter went out to churches all over the known world and taught about a myriad of subjects, such as doing good deeds, being careful about what you say, and having faith in tough times.

Discuss the passage using the following questions as a guide.

For ages 4–7
- Who can you go to for help when a bad situation happens?
- What's it like to know that God is watching over you during bad times?

For ages 8–10
- How important are friends and family during a scary situation?
- How can you rely on God during tough times?

For ages 11–13
- How can you help others through hard times?
- Can it be difficult to have faith in God during tough times? Why?

For ages 14 and up
- Why does James say to be glad during difficult times?
- How can being someone others lean on during their challenges be hard on you?

Finish your discussion with prayer, asking God to give your family faith to rely on Him and each other during difficult situations.

REACHING INTO THE WORLD

We don't have to look far to find people persevering through a crisis. Identify a person (or group of people) pushing through a life challenge. Think of some way to help that person. Perhaps someone is saddled with the responsibility of taking care of an infirmed family member . . . your family could volunteer to watch that person for a while to give the caregiver a break. Or perhaps there is a family in your community whose house burned down recently . . . you could donate clothes, toys, or household items that they might need. Look around and God will guide you to a situation where your family can be of help. After the project, say a prayer for those enduring the situation and ask for guidance in helping them in the future.

29

IN THE KNOW

Nothing is as wonderful as knowing Christ Jesus my Lord.

— PHILIPPIANS 3:8 (CEV)

There's knowing, and then there's *really* knowing. We may know our family physician, the principal at our kid's school, and the pastor of our church. We know what they look like, and we have a sense of their personalities. Yet we rarely get to know these people in a deep and intimate way that provides lasting bonds, as we do with our spouse or children or best friends. Most of us know in detail the personality traits of our good friends and family members. We know what little things irritate them, what they truly appreciate, and what they fear and why. Ideally, we deeply love them because of (and in spite of) everything we know about them, and if we're lucky, they love us the same way.

God certainly loves us that same way. He understands us beyond even what we know about ourselves. He sees all of our flaws but notices only our vast beauty. We are the recipients of love deeper than can be imagined. Part of the Christian adventure is learning more about God and growing ever deeper in our connection with Him.

REACHING IN

Hand out paper and pens or markers to everyone in your family. Give everyone a piece of paper for each person in the family (including oneself) and have him or her write each family member's name at the top of one page. Then tell your family to use what they know about each other to create a menu for a celebration feast for each person in the family. Put on the menu what you believe each person would most enjoy eating. Also be sure everyone creates a personal menu too. Young children may need some assistance. They can draw pictures of the meals in place of making a list.

Once everyone has finished, select a family member and have the others say what they think that person would put on the menu. Then have the family member reveal his or her written menu. Compare it to what everyone else put and see who comes closest. Continue with the process until everyone has taken a turn.

Debrief the exercise with the following questions:

- What did it take to do well in this game?
- What are some ways to get to know each other better?
- How would Jesus have done at this game?
- How well do you know Jesus?

We can know Jesus in the same way that we know and are known by our family members. If we want to grow in our relationship with Him, we have to keep working on knowing Him better all the time. Discuss some ways that you can get to know Jesus better.

REACHING INTO THE WORD — PHILIPPIANS 3:7-11

Read Philippians 3:7-11 to your family. This passage highlights one of Paul's themes in his letter to the church at Philippi: putting Christ first and getting to know Him more and more. Use the following questions to discuss this passage.

For ages 4–7
- What are some ways we get to know someone?
- How can we get to know God in the same way?

For ages 8–10
- How does getting to know others change a relationship?
- How can getting to know God help us love Him more?

For ages 11–13
- Why do you think Paul said that everything else besides getting to know Christ is "garbage" (cev)?
- What garbage in our lives can keep us from knowing Christ better?

For ages 14 and up
- What, if anything, do you find frightening about what Paul said in this passage?
- How can getting to know Christ better feel dangerous?

Close your family time together in prayer. Ask God to give your family the courage to keep growing in knowledge and love for Him.

REACHING INTO THE WORLD

A great way to more intimately know Jesus is to do what He did and try to put yourself in His shoes. Here's a chance for your family to mirror an action Jesus took in John 4:1-26. In Jesus' time, it was unheard of for a Jewish man to talk with a Samaritan woman. It was considered scandalous.

Identify someone in your community whom most people would ignore, look down on, or even be frightened of. Have your family strike up a conversation with that person, just as Jesus did with the Samaritan woman. Offer words of encouragement and friendship.

After you're done, pray for that person and keep in touch with him or her if possible.

30

LIVING THE TEN

And God spoke all these words: "I am the LORD your God,
who brought you out of Egypt, out of the land of slavery.
You shall have no other gods before me."

— EXODUS 20:1-3

A large percentage of Americans are into lists of advice, as evidenced by the large followings of such advice-givers as Dr. Phil, Dr. Laura, and Dave Ramsey. After all, we're busy people; we need something straightforward, something we can put on our refrigerators to remind us of our goals, priorities, or growth areas.

God provided us with a list, too—the Ten Commandments—and it cuts to the heart of every choice He directs us to make as His followers. While posting this list in our home can be a reminder of how He wants us to live, simply displaying the commandments misses the point. God didn't create them as a sign of what we believe; He gave them to Moses to help His people live. What if we took our focus off debating or talking about them? What if we just lived them?

REACHING IN

Gather at your kitchen table with paper and pen. Make a list of the Ten Commandments and let everyone study it for twenty seconds. Then hide the list and work together to recreate it from memory (don't worry about the order). Compare the list from memory with the list you studied. How did you do?

While it's not a requirement for Christians to have the Ten Commandments memorized and in order, God does want us to internalize them because they're important to our daily lives. If we live them, we'll make choices that please Him.

REACHING INTO THE WORD — EXODUS 20:1-17

The Ten Commandments is one of the best-known passages in the Bible. Why? First of all, God gave the list directly to Moses. And the commandments are clear-cut — do this, don't do that. This is good, this is bad. God laid it all out for Moses and the Israelites, and for us, too. It's our most basic list of rules for living. Read the passage and then discuss the following questions:

For ages 4–7
- What are rules for?
- What do you think God wants us to do with His commandments?

For ages 8–10
- Do you think the Ten Commandments are easy or hard? Why?
- Which one of the commandments do you have a hard time with?
- What's the point of God giving us the commandments?

For ages 11–13
- What did God mean when He commanded us not to have other gods before Him?
- How can keeping God first in our lives help us obey the Ten Commandments?
- How can you show you believe the Ten Commandments by the way you live your life? Pick a few commandments and give real-life examples.

For ages 14 and up
- How has the Ten Commandments shaped how you live your life?
- What is one commandment you feel God asking you to work on in your life?
- How can you use the Ten Commandments to help you make God-centered choices?

Close in prayer and thank God for using the Ten Commandments to help you know how to live.

REACHING INTO THE WORLD

Gather around your computer, search online for the Ten Commandments in another language that might be spoken in your community, and print it out. If you're not able to find it, seek out a friend who might be able to provide a translation in another language, and then take the translation, type it up, and print it out. Think of someone you know who speaks a different language and might like the Ten Commandments in his or her language. You could frame it and give it to that person as a gift. If you feel it's appropriate, talk about why your faith is important to you and how you wanted to share it in his or her language. You could also invite your friend to church.

If you don't think your friend would be open to hearing about your faith yet, post the Ten Commandments in his or her language in your home and pray for your friend on a daily basis—that God would help him or her learn more about Him.

31

LOOKING OUT FOR NUMBER ONE

*Religion that God our Father accepts as pure and faultless is
this: to look after orphans and widows in their distress and
to keep oneself from being polluted by the world.*

— JAMES 1:27

Here's a fun project: Go to your local bookstore, library, or favorite
online bookstore and look for self-help books. The market for them
is astounding. You'll find books on how to love yourself, communicate better, make decisions, improve your relationships; the list goes
on and on. There are books about self-coaching, ending your addiction to unhappiness, and even how to write a self-help book. These
books appeal to our desires for a better quality of life, and because
of that, they sell like hotcakes.

There's nothing wrong with wanting to better yourself;

however, we should be careful not to be so caught up in self-improvement that it gets in the way of living a God-centered life. Our first priority should be God, not ourselves. He wants us to be focused on Him, plain and simple.

REACHING IN

Plan a time for the family to get together first thing one morning. Gather in your living room or bedroom, and have everyone share his or her schedule for the day. Next, have each person think of some ways that he or she can keep God first throughout the day. Let others offer suggestions as well. Then do the "Reaching Into the Word" activity.

When your day is over and you all are around the table eating dinner, ask each person to talk about what he or she did to try to keep God first. Be sure to support, encourage, and praise each other for your family's efforts.

REACHING INTO THE WORD — JAMES 1:27

James is succinct in this verse: True religion is looking after those in need and keeping yourself from being polluted by the world. What does that have to do with keeping God first? It means that when we focus on those God loves, we are focusing on Him. Seeing those in need and being compelled to love and help them shows that we are God-focused. Discuss these questions during your early-morning time together:

For ages 4–7
- How does it feel to start the day talking about how we can put God first?

- How can God help us through our day?
- When can we think about God today?

For ages 8–10
- What did James mean when he said to "keep oneself from being polluted by the world"?
- How can we help each other keep God first today?
- How do you think it makes God feel when we put Him first?

For ages 11–13
- What things from our society or world might you like to add to James's description of pure and spotless religion? Discuss those examples with each other.
- How can you tell when someone is keeping God first in his or her day?
- How are you going to pray for someone in your family today as he or she tries to keep God first?

For ages 14 and up
- What do you think James meant by "pure and faultless religion"?
- What are some examples of that kind of religion that you see in your community or world today?
- How could a devotional time like this one help your family stay focused on God? When could you do this together again?

Pray together, asking God to help your family always stay focused on God and to show you how you can support each other as each person tries to keep Him first.

REACHING INTO THE WORLD

Find someone who is in the process of adopting a child. (If you don't know of anyone, talk with a couple who has already adopted, because they often know someone who is in the adoption process. You can also contact an adoption agency and ask if they can put you in contact with an adoptive family.) Put together a package of blessings created for the child. These can be written prayers, messages of encouragement, or pictures from your children. You can also buy a gift for the child, such as new clothes or needed baby items. Pledge to keep the family in your prayers, and then do so on a regular basis.

32

EXTINGUISHING EVIL

Do not be overcome by evil, but overcome evil with good.

— ROMANS 12:21

Those who watched *Saturday Night Live* in the late '80s and early '90s will remember Dana Carvey's unforgettable character, the "Church Lady." She would bring guests on and grill them about their sins and eventually decide that their actions were the result of . . . "Oh, I don't know, could it be, possibly . . . *Satan*?"

All kidding aside, evil has infiltrated our lives in a multitude of ways. We may not always realize it because it can be subtle. When we sin, we are choosing evil over good and allowing our sinful nature to take control of us instead of God. That kind of evil can lead us into addiction, hurting our loved ones, and bondage to sin. Evil can start out seemingly harmless and minor and grow into a huge monster. As followers of God, we're in a battle against evil, and the war isn't over until Jesus comes back for us.

REACHING IN

For this activity, gather a Bible and as many candles as you can find.

Think of some evils in the world today. They can be as big as the Holocaust or as minor as lying. Next, light a candle for each evil mentioned. Share your feelings about one or more of the evils represented, how it makes you feel or has affected you. Then tell one way you can counter that evil with good. Lighting the candle represents bringing God's light into darkness, which represents evil.

Then read Romans 12:21 and ask God to overcome those evils with good and to use your family to help. Pray a similar prayer every evening that week at dinner or family devotional time.

REACHING INTO THE WORD — ROMANS 12:21; MATTHEW 19:26

Do you sense the optimism in Jesus' words in Matthew 19:26? We must remember that, no matter the challenge, with God all things are possible. He has the power to overcome evil with good, and He can help us do the same. That includes dealing with evil actions, resisting temptation, and addressing the evil we see in the world over which we feel we have no control. Use the following questions as a guide for further discussion.

For ages 4–7
- What do you think the word *evil* means?
- When have you seen something really bad happen to someone?
- What do you think God can do about evil or bad things?

For ages 8–10

- What are some things that could be considered evil?
- What does God want us to know about evil?
- What can we do to stay away from evil?

For ages 11–13

- How can we be "overcome" by evil?
- What are some ways that we can overcome evil with good?
- What are some evils you hope God will get rid of?

For ages 14 and up

- When have you been affected or overcome by evil? What happened?
- What examples have you seen in your church or community of overcoming evil with good?
- What are some things our family can do to help obliterate an evil in the world?

Close in prayer, asking God to help your family understand your role in bringing God's light where the darkness of evil prevails.

REACHING INTO THE WORLD

As you've already discussed, the scope of evil is broader, and sometimes more subtle, than we realize. Take world hunger, for example. It's a massive negative power in our universe that continues to kill countless people who do not have enough food. While most people in the United States have food in abundance, many in the rest of the world do not.

What can we do to attack such a huge evil? Perhaps not a lot in the direct sense, other than sponsoring children in developing counties and giving to worthy charities that fight against famine. But just because we can't solve the problem doesn't mean we should do nothing.

Here's one more way your family can help: Go to www.thehungersite.com. Each time a person visits this site, the sponsors donate money to feed the hungry in a foreign country. Add this site to your favorites, and go there each time you're on the Internet. Make this a part of your daily routine, and you will contribute to making a difference in the battle against the evil of world hunger.

33

THE BIG FEAR FACE-OFF

So do not fear, for I am with you; do not be dismayed,
for I am your God. I will strengthen you and help you;
I will uphold you with my righteous right hand.

— ISAIAH 41:10

While many of the things we are afraid of—getting kicked off the team, getting an F on our report card, getting laid off from our job—are more worries than actual reality, sometimes our worse fears do come true. What then? What if our reality *is* scary and there is no way out except to go through the scary situation? What do we do when a loved one has cancer? Or we're overwhelmed by debt, with no savings to fall back on? Or when we're being persecuted for what we believe in?

God is with us throughout the fears of life, but can He really help us when we're facing such fears? Yes, He can. But what might surprise you is that He might expect you to stand and fight that fear—because He knows you can (even if you think you can't). That's what this mission is all about: believing that we can face our fears, and that God helps us do just that.

REACHING IN

Gather your family in your backyard at night with a flashlight, or if you're doing this activity around Halloween, you could wear costumes. Take a picture of each person's scariest face. If you have access to a printer, print out the pictures (you could put them on your fridge later to remind you of your time together), or just look at them on the camera.

Next, have each person name some of his or her fears. Remind everyone that it is okay to say what our fears are, because we all have them and everyone understands what it's like to be scared.

Then have family members pick one fear and share a time that it kept them from doing something they wanted to do. For example, maybe you love to sing, but you're afraid of getting up in front of a crowd. Or maybe you wanted to meet a new friend at school, but you were afraid of what people would think so you didn't introduce yourself to him or her.

Then share a time when a fear kept you from doing something you knew God wanted you to do. Maybe He wanted you to invite someone to church, but you were afraid of what that person would think or say so you didn't do it.

Fear paralyzes us. We get so wrapped up in what we're afraid of that we can't move. Fear can even make us feel sick to our stomachs. How do you deal with fear? Do you get angry, cry, hide, or avoid the situation? Give everyone a chance to give his or her answers.

REACHING INTO THE WORD — ISAIAH 41:10-13; JONAH 1–4

God asked Jonah to go to Ninevah and tell the people that God wanted them to obey Him. But Jonah was scared, so he tried to hide from God and ended up in the belly of a whale. While there, he realized he had disobeyed God. So he prayed and agreed to do what God asked. The whale spit Jonah back out, and he went to Ninevah and took care of God's business.

So often in life we are afraid, and our gut reaction is to run. We might tell ourselves things like, "I can't do that," "That's too much for me," "I don't know how." We hate the discomfort of fear so much that we'll justify not having to face it in any way we can.

Life is not always going to be comfortable. Sometimes we have to leave our comfort zones and do something difficult. As Jonah discovered, when God asks us to do that, He has a good reason for it. He knows what's best for us. That's why He promised to strengthen us as we face our fears (see Isaiah 41:10).

Read the two Scripture passages and then use the following questions for more discussion.

For ages 4–7
- What's one thing you're scared of doing?
- How can God help you with that fear?
- What's one thing you used to be afraid of that you're not afraid of anymore? Why aren't you afraid of it anymore?

For ages 8–10
- What do you think would happen if you did something you're afraid of?

- How does it make you feel to know that God is with you in the scary times?

For ages 11–13
- What's your reaction to fear? Do you stay and fight? Run away? Cry? Avoid it?
- When have you felt God asking you to do something that seemed scary?
- How does doing what we're afraid of make us stronger?

For ages 14 and up
- What does it mean to you to face your fear?
- What's one fear you struggle with right now?
- What are some things you can do to deal with that fear and not run from it?

Pray together, asking God to help you not be afraid and rely on Him in scary times.

REACHING INTO THE WORLD

We often think that if we're afraid of something, there must be a good reason for it and we should avoid the situation. Our instincts tell us to run away. It might be dangerous. But sometimes — if we'll let it — the discomfort of fear helps us grow. This activity will help your family learn just a little bit about what that means.

Together, make a healthy meal and pack it along with utensils, a Bible, and the name and address of a church or homeless shelter. Go to a place in your community where you are likely to find a homeless person, and give the meal and other items to someone who fits that criterion. Pray for God to show you which person to choose. Even if the person looks scary, keep in mind that he or she might be someone who needs your care package the most; ask God to give you the strength to overcome your fear so that you can reach out to the person in need. Then commit to praying regularly for that person.

34

LEAVING YOUR LIGHTS ON

In the same way, let your light shine before men,
that they may see your good deeds and
praise your Father in heaven.

— MATTHEW 5:16

Everyone needs light. Studies have shown that if we don't get enough sunlight, it can cause depression. In the same way, people need the light of Jesus in their lives. As the popular children's song says—"This little light of mine, I'm gonna let it shine . . ."—we shouldn't hide the light of Christ. We should let it shine brightly so that everyone can see. Jesus has chosen us to bring His light to a dark world.

Even though this is a simple message, it doesn't mean it's easy to let our light shine. We may buckle under the world's pressure to act a certain way or lose sight of the importance of sharing our light with others. As you focus on letting your light shine, consider how you can avoid the obstacles that block others' view of your light.

REACHING IN

Do this activity at dusk or at night. Get a flashlight and a Bible, turn off all the lights in your house, then go outside and look at your house while one person reads Matthew 5:13-16. Discuss what it means to let our light shine. How do we do that?

Next, go into your dark house together. Turn on each light, and as you do, name a person you know who lets his or her light shine. Do this until all the lights are on. When you're done, go back outside and look at your house with all the lights on. Pray together for all the people you mentioned and also ask God to help your family be a light for Jesus.

REACHING INTO THE WORD — MATTHEW 5:13-16

Salt and light . . . what do these two things mean for us as Christians? Salt preserves and flavors, and light reveals. Think about that imagery for a moment. We are called to be salt and light. God wants us to preserve the faith and make our presence as Christ's followers known to as many people as we can. How are you like salt and light? Where are those things in your life? Everything we do should come back to that basic desire God has for us to be salt and light. Read these verses and then ask the following questions:

For ages 4–7
- Who told you about Jesus?

- Who can you tell about Jesus?
- How does it make God feel when we tell others about Him?

For ages 8–10
- How is telling others about Jesus like letting a light shine?
- Why does God want us to share Jesus with others?
- How can you share Jesus with others?

For ages 11–13
- What do you think it means to be salt and light as Christians?
- What has Jesus done for you that you want to share with others?
- How can you let your light shine at school? With friends? In sports?

For ages 14 and up
- In Matthew 5:14, what did Jesus mean when He said, "A city on a hill cannot be hidden"?
- What are some ways you think others can tell that you believe in Jesus?
- What are some changes you can make in your life so that your light shines brighter?

Close in prayer, asking God to give you the courage to shine Jesus' light everywhere you go.

REACHING INTO THE WORLD

Wherever we are and whatever we are doing, we can share the light of Christ. But we can also make an effort to share the light of Jesus in places where we might not normally go.

Set a time for your family to go to a nursing home or assisted-living center and visit with the residents there. Contact the administrator ahead of time to be sure it's okay to visit. Also, ask if you can bring a camera to take pictures of the residents with your family. (An instant-print camera would work best so you can leave pictures with the residents.) If you can't take photos, prepare a special gift for the residents (such as potpourri or flowers). You'll also want to take a Bible along.

When you visit with the residents, be sure to allow them time to talk and share with you about their lives; listen patiently. You could also ask if they have any favorite Bible passages they would like to hear, and read them aloud. Also before you leave, if you feel comfortable doing so, ask if you can pray with them.

35

GIVING THANKS, SHOWING THANKS

Come, let us sing for joy to the LORD; let us shout aloud to the Rock of our salvation. Let us come before him with thanksgiving and extol him with music and song.

— PSALM 95:1-2

Have you ever noticed that the more thankful you are, the more you find to be thankful for? When we are thankful, it affects the way we see life. It shows us the positives of life amidst the negatives and opens up our hearts to more gratitude. It takes the focus off our problems and turns it outward to the bigger picture and, ultimately, to our Creator. Gratitude is indeed powerful.

When was the last time you told someone how much you appreciate him or her? Do your loved ones know that you're thankful for them? Let's focus on what it means to be thankful and what it means to show it with our lives.

REACHING IN

Gather in your favorite spot—your living room, backyard, favorite restaurant, or the woods. Sit in a circle together. Stay silent for a few minutes and enjoy your favorite place.

Next, go around the circle and have each person name one thing he or she is thankful for that begins with a letter of the alphabet. Go in order, starting with A, until you've gone through the entire alphabet. Then have everyone identify one thing about each family member that they are thankful for.

It's important for families to regularly spend time encouraging and expressing gratitude for each other. Daily life can take a toll on each of us, and we need to be able to come back to a support system that lifts us up. Consider how you can make this activity a regular part of your family time.

REACHING INTO THE WORD—PSALM 95:1-7

Psalm 95 invites the reader to praise God for taking care of His people. Praise and thanksgiving go hand in hand. When we praise God, we acknowledge the good things He's done. We honor Him for being powerful and great. Isn't that like being thankful, too? Being thankful for God is a way to praise and honor His name because it recognizes His presence, power, and goodness.

In all that you do, be thankful to God for what He does for you. Praise Him in everything, and you'll cultivate a thankful heart that recognizes blessings. Reflect on the following questions as a family:

For ages 4–7

- What do we say when someone does something nice for us?
- What do you think it means to be thankful?
- What are you thankful for?

For ages 8–10

- Why is it hard at times to be thankful?
- Who do you need to thank for the things they do for you?

For ages 11–13

- When you praise someone, what are you doing for him or her?
- Who in your family would you praise? Why?
- Why is it important that we let people know when we are thankful for them?

For ages 14 and up

- Who do you think might be thankful for you? Why?
- How thankful would you say you are today?
- How might it change tomorrow if you have a more thankful attitude?

Pray together, asking God to guide you to be full of gratitude and thankfulness every day.

REACHING INTO THE WORLD

Have everyone in your family go through his or her toys, clothes, and any other belongings, looking for things to give away to someone else who needs them. Plan to take them to The Salvation Army or another local charity that distributes gently used items for free. Do this as a family and, on your way to deliver these items, discuss together how the act of giving your things to others is an act of gratitude and thankfulness. We have so much, but others have so little. By sharing your things with them, you show gratitude to God for the many ways He takes care of you.

Another variation of this activity is to get a few families together and organize a multifamily "store" with donated items, and then invite people in need to come through your "store" and shop for free. This can be set up at a local church or even in someone's garage.

36

ENEMY LOVE

*But I tell you: Love your enemies and pray for those
who persecute you, that you may be sons of your Father
in heaven. He causes his sun to rise on the evil and the good,
and sends rain on the righteous and the unrighteous.*

— MATTHEW 5:44-45

Loving our enemies is an extreme act, perhaps the most extreme act Jesus has ever required of His followers. It's just plain *hard* to love the people we don't like. It goes against our instincts. It makes us feel vulnerable. But it's at the core of who we are as believers. We are new creations in Christ because He loved us — even though we're sinners. So we should love others, no matter what they do to us. We're all imperfect. We all do wrong things, and we all need forgiveness.

To whom in your life do you struggle to give "enemy love"? Whom do you have a hard time forgiving? Whom do you just not like? That's the person you need to love.

REACHING IN

Some things make a great pair: peanut butter and jelly, movies and popcorn, pearls and an evening gown, and a crisp fall day and a game of backyard football with friends. Send your family on a search in your house for things that go together. Give everyone five minutes to find one or two pairs and bring them back to share with the group.

After you're done sharing the pairs you found, mix them up so that nothing goes together. Maybe pearls and peanut butter, or a remote control and tennis shoes. Make each new pair as mismatched as possible.

Could your new pairs ever go together? Share your thoughts with each other.

Next, ask each person to talk about someone he or she doesn't like, or a time when it was hard to get along with someone, and how he or she dealt with that person.

Finally, think about things that each person could do to love that "enemy."

As you move into the "Reaching Into the Word" section, think about why it is important to love those people we find hard to love.

REACHING INTO THE WORD — MATTHEW 5:43-47

There are so many fantastic ideas in these verses. First, Jesus said that we should love our enemies (just like He did). He also told us to pray for those who hurt us (just like He would do). He reminded us that God's love (like the sun and the rain) is extended to both the righteous and the unrighteous. And He went on to say that we should love when it's hard—and not just when it's easy. He finished by challenging us to be perfect, just like Him.

Do you see the theme here? We should love everyone, even those whom we dislike. Even those who hurt us. Especially those who drive us into the ground. Just as Jesus loved His enemies right through the moment when they killed Him, He wants us to do the same. Jesus wants our love to consistently go *that far*. Consider the following questions about love:

For ages 4–7
- What does it mean to love someone?
- What is an enemy?
- Why does Jesus want us to love everyone, even enemies?

For ages 8–10
- What did Jesus say to do for those who persecute or hurt us?
- How can it help when we pray for our enemies?
- How can we show love for our enemies?

For ages 11–13
- Matthew 5:38 says that we should go beyond loving those who are easy to love. What good can come from loving when it's hard?
- Do you think it's easy or hard for Jesus to love us sometimes? Explain your answer.

For ages 14 and up
- Jesus said that God makes the sun rise and the rain fall on the evil and the good. What do you think He was saying about God?

- How is a new day or a nurturing rain like God telling us He loves us?
- Does it change the way you view your enemies to know that God loves them, too? Why or why not?
- Why does God give us the chance of another day to do the right thing?

Close in prayer, asking God to help your family love the people they have a difficult time loving.

REACHING INTO THE WORLD

Ask each person in your family to think about this question: Whom might you consider your enemy? Maybe it's someone that you just don't like or a friend you're having some disagreements with.

Next, go shopping together for your enemies. Have each person pick out a small gift and a card for his or her enemy. When you get back home, take time helping each other write a kind note in the cards for your enemies. Because the relationships may be different, you'll want to consider what kind of personalized note to write.

Finally, find the time in the next few days to deliver the gifts to the people you've selected. It doesn't have to be a long conversation, just a friendly moment. As you do it, think about how much Jesus loves that person, and pray that God will help you show that love to him or her.

37

PASS THE PEACE

*Glory to God in the highest, and on earth peace to men
on whom his favor rests.*

— LUKE 2:14

There's an ancient folktale about two brothers. One decided to stay in the village and spend his life eking out a living by fishing every day and living a quiet existence. His brother decided to go off to the city and spend his years building a fortune. He worked day and night, struggling and fighting his way to the top. One day the successful brother was asked, "Why did you spend your life struggling to make a fortune?" He replied, "So that one day I could settle down, fish every day, and live a quiet existence."

This folktale teaches just how simple peace really is. We rush around trying to get everything in order so that we can settle down, when what we really need to do is rest in the peace of Christ right now. Jesus' peace gives us hope for eternity. But we should not forget that Jesus also gives us peace from the daily grind of life. Read on to find out more about how Jesus and peace go hand in hand.

REACHING IN

Since life brings a full schedule comprised of travel, school events, church, and work, your family will have to be intentional if you want to experience some relaxing peace. Block out a few hours, perhaps an afternoon or evening to relax together. Rent a movie, order dinner, and have it delivered to you. Make the time together as simple and easy as possible.

At some point in your time together, discuss this question: What changes can we make in our schedule so that our family experiences more peacefulness?

Commit together to cut back on the stress and foster more peace in your family's activities.

REACHING INTO THE WORD — LUKE 2:14

When Jesus was born, the course of the world changed. This verse reminds us of the magnitude of that moment. The angels, who said these words in praise to God for His Son, knew that God had just given the ultimate gift to every human being. In His great power and love, God sent His Son to the earth to show people what He wants us to do with our lives, to tell people how they can be in fellowship with God once again, and to ultimately show us what God is like "with skin on."

Look at the second part of that verse, though: "Peace to men on whom his favor rests." What could that mean? Perhaps it means that for those who believe in Jesus and give their lives to Him, there is a peace that overrides life's struggles. Not just a calmness, or a smile on our faces, but a deep sense of peace. Because Jesus is finally here, we are victorious over death and will someday transcend that hurdle and experience eternal life with God. What else could we say? *Glory to God* indeed.

Use the following questions as a guide to discuss this further.

For ages 4–7

- Why do you think God gave us Jesus?
- What does it mean to have peace?

For ages 8–10

- In Luke 2:14, the angels said, "Glory to God!" How might you express your thanks to God if Jesus had just come and you witnessed it?
- Why is peace so important?
- When have you felt peace? What did it feel like?

For ages 11–13

- What are some things that rob us of our peace?
- What can you do to help people see how Jesus gives us peace?
- What one person do you especially hope finds more peace in his or her life?

For ages 14 and up

- Luke 2:14 says, "Peace to men on whom his favor rests." What do you think that means?
- When have you experienced peace in a time of difficulty or stress? Talk about that experience.

- How can you help others have more peace?
- Whom would you like to reach out to with the peace of Jesus?

Close in prayer, asking God to help you cultivate peace year-round.

REACHING INTO THE WORLD

Go to a craft store and get some foam or cardboard door hangers that can be decorated. (Or you can easily make your own with poster board. Cut out a foot-long rectangle and a hole near the top that's big enough to fit around a doorknob.) You might purchase several so you can make enough for a few friends or neighbors. You'll also need decorating supplies. You can use anything you like — stickers, craft jewels, paint, markers, ribbons, and so on.

Decorate the door hangers with a focus on peace. You could write: "From the _____ family . . . we wish you peace." Also include decorations that remind you of peace. Those could be a dove, a cross, or whatever else symbolizes peace for you. You could also include the Scripture verse, Luke 2:14.

Before delivering the door hangers, say a prayer for the recipients, that God would give them peace through Jesus.

38

THE GUIDE INSIDE

But the Counselor, the Holy Spirit, whom the Father
will send in my name, will teach you all things and
will remind you of everything I have said to you.
Peace I leave with you; my peace I give you. I do not give
to you as the world gives. Do not let your hearts be troubled
and do not be afraid.

— JOHN 14:26-27

If you've ever taken a trip using a global positioning system (GPS), you know that when you don't take the suggested route, it will politely inform you of your mistake and try to get you back on track. When Jesus went back to heaven, God sent us the Holy Spirit to serve as our GPS — to give us direction, help us understand what God wants us to do as we navigate through life.

The Holy Spirit will influence our convictions, decision-making, and thought processes. He is our guide. For instance, when you're reading the Bible and feel that God is speaking to you through a certain verse, the Holy Spirit is involved in that realization. When your gut tells you to invite your friend to church on Sunday, the Holy Spirit might be giving you direction.

REACHING IN

Gather everyone by the front door of your home and have them pair up. (If you have an uneven number, ask someone to volunteer to do this activity twice.) Have one person close his or her eyes and be "blind," while the other person is the guide.

Have the guides lead the blind people around the house by whispering directions in the blind person's ear. The guides can't touch or pull the blind person. When the pairs are finished, have each person switch roles.

When everyone has been both a guide and a blind person, come back together to talk about your experiences.

- What did it feel like to be led by the guide?
- What did it feel like to lead your partner with whispered directions?
- Was it easy or difficult?

Finally, have everyone share his or her thoughts on the Holy Spirit and what He does. How might this activity be like listening to the Holy Spirit? In what ways could that be similar to how the Holy Spirit leads us through life? Give everyone time to share his or her thoughts.

REACHING INTO THE WORD — JOHN 14:15-31

The Holy Spirit plays an integral role as you live out your faith on a daily basis. Sometimes people see the Holy Spirit as an element of Christian faith that we know is there but don't know much about.

In this passage, we're told the Holy Spirit is our guide, companion, counsel, and go-between. He's the gentle nudge in a decision and the still small voice when we are grappling with doing the right thing. He's our hand-holder, so we're not alone as we walk through life. He reminds us to love God with our lives, helps us make God-honoring decisions, and comforts us with God's love when we struggle with challenges.

After you read the passage, discuss the following questions:

For ages 4–7
- How does it make you feel when you have a friend with you?
- How is the Holy Spirit like a friend?
- Why did God give us the Holy Spirit?

For ages 8–10
- In John 14:16-17, how did Jesus describe the Holy Spirit?
- According to Jesus' words, how can the Holy Spirit help us?
- Have you ever felt the Holy Spirit helping you? Talk about that experience.

For ages 11–13
- What does John 14:25-26 say about the job of the Holy Spirit?

- When have you felt the Holy Spirit doing that for you? Talk about that experience.
- How can the Holy Spirit help you with the choices you face in life?

For ages 14 and up
- In John 14, what is similar about verses 19-21 and verse 31?
- How can the Holy Spirit help us obey God?
- What things can our family do to become more aware of the Holy Spirit's leading in your life?

Pray together and ask God to help your family be guided by the Holy Spirit as He gives direction for your lives.

REACHING INTO THE WORLD

Is there a missions idea that has been on your heart for a while? During a family meal or a fun night out to eat, have family members share ideas they've had about new missions opportunities and talk about whether that might be the Holy Spirit leading your family to do something about one of them (or more!). In your regular prayer time together, ask God if your family is being led to take action on something, and listen to the Holy Spirit. The practice of listening in prayer is an important skill. You may have to explain to your younger children that God doesn't speak in an audible voice, but rather to our hearts in a way that we'll understand.

When you've decided on something you feel the Holy Spirit is guiding you to do together as a family, pray about it before, during, and after the mission. Not only is this a chance to do something good for others, it's also a chance to learn more about what it means to follow the voice of the Holy Spirit as we do God's work.

39

OPEN HOUSE

But the angel said to them, "Do not be afraid.
I bring you good news of great joy that will be
for all the people. Today in the town of David a Savior
has been born to you; he is Christ the Lord."

— LUKE 2:10-11

All around the world at Christmastime, people celebrate in unique ways. For example, in Italy they create beautiful and elaborate manger scenes everywhere you look. In Poland they celebrate with the oplatki wafer, similar to a communion wafer but etched with intricate Christmas designs, which they pass around to loved ones and share a blessing with the person it is passed to. In Guatemala they have a special tradition called "Misa de Gallo" (Mass of the Rooster) at midnight on Christmas Eve, based on a Guatemalan legend that says a rooster crowed at midnight when Christ was born.

There are so many different traditions, practices, and

memorable stories that we enjoy this time of year. As Christ followers, regardless of our traditions, one of the best things about Christmas is celebrating Christ together. Christmas is a time for families and friends to reunite, but it can also be a time to form new friendships and help others who might be on the fringe of family celebrations be a part of what you're doing at Christmas.

REACHING IN

If you have a fireplace, this is a great activity to do sitting around the fire with hot chocolate and cookies. You'll also need a Bible, index cards, paper, pens, and a paper sack.

If you haven't done anything to commemorate the season yet, here's an opportunity for you to do that. As you sit around the fire, read Luke 2:1-20 (the Christmas story). If your children want to, encourage them to take turns reading the story out loud.

Next, discuss these questions together:

- Why do people give gifts to each other at Christmas?
- What do you hope the other people will think when they get your gifts?
- How can you be a gift to each other at Christmas?

Share ideas of things you can do for each other that are helpful and loving—and that could be a "gift" to someone else.

Finally, have each family member write his or her name on a piece of paper, fold it up, and put it in a paper sack. Once all the names are in the bag, have each person draw someone else's name. That person is who you'll shower with gifts of love, kindness, and helpfulness this Christmas. Once you've drawn names, make a list of some things you can do for that person in the next week. Keep the list in a place that will remind you to give the gift of yourself.

REACHING INTO THE WORD — LUKE 2:1-20

You've already read the Christmas story together as a family in the "Reaching In" section. Make this a time to focus on how the message of Christmas can be extended to others. In the passage, the angel Gabriel spoke to the shepherds in the fields and told them to go see the baby Jesus, the Savior of the world. In our world today, the invitation is still necessary. There are countless millions who still need to go see Jesus. Reflect on who in your world still needs to see Him.

Use the following questions as a guide to discuss this in more detail.

For ages 4–7
- Why do we celebrate Christmas?
- What did Jesus do for us?
- How is Jesus a gift to us from God?

For ages 8–10
- If you were a shepherd, what would you have thought when an angel appeared to you?
- What tradition at Christmas helps you focus on Jesus?
- What new things could you do to focus on Jesus this Christmas?

For ages 11–13
- What's the most memorable Christmas you've had so far? Share about that time.

- What was the shepherds' response after the angel spoke to them (see verse 15)?
- How does it make you feel to know that Jesus is God's gift to you?
- How can you extend that gift to someone else?

For ages 14 and up
- After the shepherds saw the baby Jesus, what did they do (see verses 17-18)?
- Whom are you sharing the Good News with this Christmas?
- What are some changes you can make to your Christmas celebrations so they are more Jesus-focused and an opportunity to reach out to others?

Pray together and ask God to show you someone you can open your house to and include in your Christmas celebration.

REACHING INTO THE WORLD

At Christmas we open our doors to family and friends, and all our loved ones are represented around our trees and dining-room tables. But what about those who have to spend Christmas alone? Do you know someone who might be lonely at Christmas?

Invite that person to your house for Christmas. Buy gifts for him or her and put them under your tree. When that individual comes over, make him or her a part of your family. Include him or her in your festivities; spend time talking with and listening to that person. Send your guest home with packages and extra food to remember the day.

You may never know how much this could be a blessing to your guest. Allow the warmth of your family to extend beyond your front door, and you'll give a gift this Christmas that surpasses anything wrapped underneath your tree.

40

THE NEVER-ENDING ADVENTURE

Bring the best of the firstfruits of your soil to the house of the LORD your God.

— EXODUS 23:19

Have you ever known people who sit around and complain about being bored or having a life that is too routine? Normally, adventure doesn't just happen upon us; we have to go find it. As Christians, Jesus has adventures for us all the time, but we have to be looking for them. When we do, we'll be amazed at the ways our family will put its mark on the world for Jesus.

Jesus was always others-oriented. He spent His life showing people who God was. If we want to take those adventures with Him, we also need to be willing to bring others along with us. We'll be glad we did, and so will our family and friends, both old and new.

God is ready to use families for opportunities to honor Him and accomplish His purpose here on earth. God wants us to contribute to His work in many ways.

REACHING IN

You'll need a bank or container that holds both coins and bills, some poster board, markers, craft supplies such as stickers and glitter glue, tape, and a Bible.

Sit around the kitchen table with a Bible, poster board, and markers. Think about people in the Bible who served God. Young children could draw pictures of Bible stories on the poster board; older kids could write out their examples. Find where those stories are in the Bible and take turns reading them aloud (younger children who aren't yet reading could recount the story as they remember it).

Next, tell each other some ways you have seen people serving God and others in your church, community, nation, or world in the past year. (Younger children can draw pictures on the poster board; older children can write their ideas.)

Finally, think of some ways that each of you has served God, and share, draw, or write out your examples. Look at your collage of serving God. What's your favorite example from the Bible? What's an example from the world around you that's had an effect on you? What's one example from someone in your family that you like? Share your thoughts with each other.

Turn the poster board over. Here you'll create a giving plan for your family. The idea of a family giving plan is to help you organize how you'll give to God throughout the year and stay accountable to what you've promised to do.

First, write these headings along the top of your poster board: Time, Resources, Relationships, and Prayer. Draw lines in between the headings that go down the page to create columns.

Next, brainstorm some ideas for giving under each of these headers. For example, under "Money" you might list a certain amount of money that you will put in the bank or container per week or per month, and your children may list a certain amount out of their allowance each week to go into the bank or container. Under "Time" you might list helping out in the local food pantry every Saturday, or helping a family find clothing or resources by talking with them about their needs and then bringing donations to them. Under "Relationships" you might list names of people you would like to share the love of Christ with, and under "Prayer" you might list people and concerns you can pray for.

If you think your younger kids will get antsy while you brainstorm, ask for their suggestions first; then get them started on decorating the bank using the craft supplies.

Once you've finished your giving plan and your bank, set them where everyone can see them, such as in your kitchen. Take the money from it on the first Sunday of every month and give it to your church or another worthy cause that you've designated in your plan.

REACHING INTO THE WORD — EXODUS 23:19

When we make lists of things we need to get done, we usually put the most important job, the one we want to finish first, at the top. When we visit an amusement park, we often want to go on our favorite ride first, right? We know what's most important to us, and we give that our full attention. God wants us to do the same in our relationship with Him. He wants us to make giving to Him our top priority. After all, He provides everything we need. We have Him to thank for all the things we have and the gifts He has given us.

Our Bible verse comes from the book of Exodus, the story of Moses leading the people of Israel away from slavery in Egypt. In chapter 20, God gave Moses the Ten Commandments at Mount Sinai, and for the remainder of the book, God set down rules for the community to live by.

Our Scripture verse is one of those rules, found in Exodus 23:19. "Firstfruits" refers to farmers giving the best part of their crop or harvest to God. Read the verse together and discuss these questions:

For ages 4–7
- What's your favorite fruit? Why?
- Would you give some of your favorite fruit to someone else if he or she asked? Why or why not?
- If someone else had some of your favorite fruit, would you want that person to give some to you?

For ages 8–10
- What if you were to give away a favorite toy or gift to another child who had no toys—would that be easy or hard?
- What do you think firstfruits are?

For ages 11–13
- What are some of your firstfruits?
- Why does God want you to give your firstfruits to Him?

- Do you think it would be easy or difficult to give them to Him? Why?

For ages 14 and up
- When has someone given you their firstfruits, and how did that feel?
- What are the firstfruits of your family?
- What could happen when we give God our firstfruits of time, money, and other things?
- Why might people not give their firstfruits?

Next, pray together. Commit your family's firstfruits and giving plan to God. God can take your willingness to serve Him and turn it into an amazing adventure. Remember that if you are willing, God is ready to use you. Ask Him to take control and use your efforts to do His work.

Praying together will not only strengthen your family bond, it will make everyone feel a part of something special. And it will help your kids feel more comfortable praying out loud.

REACHING INTO THE WORLD

Get started with one thing on your giving plan. Pick something from one of the categories that all of you can do together. As you tackle the things on your plan, you may want to take pictures of each activity you do together and keep the pictures in a photo album as a reminder of how your family worked together.

As you embark on these adventures, take time to marvel at the beautiful family God has blessed you with. Thank God for the opportunity to build bonds together as you embrace His world.

NOTES

Chapter 7. Time Out . . . It's Prayer Time

1. Jack Wintz, O.F.M., "Family Theater at 50: Father Patrick Peyton Remembered," *St. Anthony Messenger*, June 1997, http://www.americancatholic.org/Messenger/Jun1997/feature2.asp.

Chapter 13. Forgiveness House

1. "On the Road to Democracy," The Truth & Reconciliation Commission, http://www.sahistory.org.za/pages/governence-projects/TRC/index.htm.

Chapter 19. Downtime

1. J. Christian Gillin, "How Long Can Humans Stay Awake," *Scientific American*, March 25, 2002, http://www.scientificamerican.com/article.cfm?id=how-long-can-humans-stay.

Chapter 20. You're Never Out

1. Philip Yancey, *What's So Amazing About Grace?* (Grand Rapids, MI: Zondervan, 1997), 45.

Chapter 25. We Got Gifts!

1. Found at http://www.guinnessworldrecords.com.

ABOUT THE AUTHORS

TIM SIMPSON has served as an education minister and a children's ministry worker for more than twenty years. He holds master's degrees in education (University of Kentucky) and Christian education (Southern Seminary in Louisville, Kentucky).

ALISON SIMPSON is an accomplished writer of youth and children's curriculum, Bible studies, and devotional materials for all ages. She has been a contributing writer for publishers such as Group Publishing, Gospel Light, and David C. Cook. She holds a degree in journalism from Asbury College in Wilmore, Kentucky. Tim, Alison, and their two children live in Frankfort.

More great NavPress products for children!

My First Message
Eugene H. Peterson
978-1-57683-448-0

This one-of-a-kind Bible transforms family devotionals into interactive experiences. The beloved *Message* style offers a version that is easy to read and understand. Young children will be encouraged to learn to study the Bible through the read, think, pray, and live approach. This Bible is full of lively illustrations and fun activities for parents and children.

Praying Through the Bible with My First Message
Pray! Magazine
978-1-60006-204-9

Help your children learn how to powerfully pray Scripture. Use these colorful new kids' prayer cards in conjunction with *My First Message* or with any easy-to-understand Bible translation. Teach your children to pray through the Bible themselves with fifty different Scripture-based prayers in this five-card set.

T.H.U.M.B. Prayer Cards
Pray! Magazine
978-1-60006-119-6

T.H.U.M.B. prayer cards teach kids to pray for tribal, Hindu, unreligious, Muslim, and Buddhist peoples around the world. Each pack contains five cards plus a guide for parents and teachers.

To see more prayer cards from Pray! Magazine, go to www.navpress.com.
To order copies, call NavPress at 1-800-366-7788 or log on to www.navpress.com.

NAVPRESS

Discipleship Inside Out™

Experience more quality time with your children!

201 Great Questions for Parents and Children
Jerry D. Jones

This easy-to-use tool helps parents interact with their children to build mutual understanding and deeper family relationships. From simple questions about dreams and personal interpretations to deeper questions about life values, this book will help both parents and children learn to communicate effectively with each other. Useful with children of all ages living at home.

978-1-57683-147-2

Prayer-Saturated Kids
Cheryl Sacks and Arlyn Lawrence

Practical help and inspiring real-life stories will equip you to teach and mentor children to become powerful lifelong pray-ers while your own prayer life is growing right along with theirs

978-1-60006-136-3

Creative Family Prayer Times
Mike and Amy Nappa

Creative Family Prayer Times is a collection of fifty-two innovative prayer ideas to help you add meaning to family devotions. Divided into daily, monthly, and yearly activities, these hands-on, creative ideas will bring a change of pace to what you already do during family prayer.

978-1-60006-257-5